To my favorite storytellers: Jo, Katie, and Orrin

Lectionary Stories Cycle B

40 Tellable Stories for Advent, Christmas, Epiphany, Lent, Easter and Pentecost

By John E. Sumwalt

C.S.S. Publishing Co.
Lima, Ohio

Reprinted 1993

Third Printing 1991
Second Printing 1991

Copyright © 1990 by
The C.S.S. Publishing Company, Inc.
Lima, Ohio

All stories and characters depicted in this book are fictitious except for those in the chapters titled ''Diane's Story,'' ''Home Town Apocalypse,'' and ''The Most Pop in the County.''

Library of Congress Cataloging-in-Publication Data

Sumwalt, John.
    Lectionary stories. Cycle B : 40 tellable stories for Advent,
Christmas, Epiphany, Lent, Easter, and Pentecost / by John Sumwalt.
        p.   cm.
    ISBN 1-55673-244-9
    1. Homiletical illustrations. 2. Common lectionary. 3. Bible-
Homiletical use. I. Title.
BV4225.2.S955 1990
251'.08—dc20
                                                                    90-41530
                                                                        CIP

9057 / ISBN 1-55673-244-9

PRINTED IN U.S.A.

Acknowledgements

My thanks to Richard Steele, Kathleen Thompson, Mary Norris, Sue D'Alessio, Steve Zekoff, Jane Follmer Zekoff, Susan Patterson-Sumwalt and Jo Perry-Sumwalt, for reading and critiquing portions of the manuscript. To Michael Williams, Dave Kruse, Frank Gaylord, Lucretia Fehrmann, Don Fenner, Jay Smoke and Jerry Shenk, I offer my deep appreciation for their encouragement and support. Special thanks to Donna Jones and Dave Hackamack for typing and computer programming assistance.

To my parents, Leonard and Bernice Sumwalt, my grandmothers, Leona Amanda Long, and Nellie Jane Kittle Sumwalt, I am grateful for all the stories I heard snuggled on their laps as a child. In the family and biblical stories they read and told I came to know myself as part of God's continuing story.

My special thanks to the congregations of Trinity United Methodist Church in Montello, Cargill United Methodist Church in Janesville, and Wesley United Methodist Church in Kenosha, who have both suffered and rejoiced with me in the birthing of these stories.

Contents

The Power of Stories

The task of the preacher is to hold life up to us, by whatever gifts he or she has of imagination, eloquence, simple candor, to create images of life through which we can somehow see into the wordless truth of our lives. [1]

Frederick Buechner

One good way, perhaps one of the best ways, of seeing into "the wordless truth of our lives," [2] is through the telling and hearing of stories. Since I have begun to tell stories in my sermons, I have discovered that I receive a different kind of response than to more conventional kinds of preaching. People come up to me after the service and instead of saying "that was a good sermon" or "I appreciated what you had to say today," they tell me one of their own stories. Sometimes this occurs weeks or even months afterwards. Stories are remembered and pondered for a long time.

Stories work in our unconscious minds slowly over time, gradually mixing with our own ideas and memories, healing our spirits as we absorb their truths. They help us to know things about ourselves, our relationships with others, the nature of the universe and our God that we could not discover in any other way. A story in which someone is redeemed, set free from some affliction or sin, will often function redemptively in the life of the hearer. Fred Craddock writes in *Overhearing the Gospel*, that ". . . a narrative tends to do what it tells, mediating suffering and healing and salvation." [3]

Unfortunately, as Michael Goldberg points out in *Theology and Narrative*, "Nowadays for many the word 'story' connotes something fictitious, something not to be taken seriously, something which serves as an aid to the intellectually unsophisticated, who, had they sufficient powers of discursive reasoning, could simply dispense with these figurative ways of presenting abstract ideas."[4] I feel this sometimes when I tell stories for the first time in a new congregation or to a secular audience that is not accustomed to hearing stories. They may allow themselves to be entertained by the stories, they may laugh or even cry, but the unspoken, perhaps unconscious response is a reluctance to enter fully into the stories. Through their facial expressions and other body language they say they are not sure if listening to stories is a legitimate adult activity. Michael Williams writes in *Friends For Life*, that "Many of us suffer from the misunderstanding that stories are just for children, that we grow out of a need to hear them."[5] Even biblical stories, including the parables of Jesus, are dismissed by some as 'just stories'. Thomas Boomershine says in a *Story Journey*, "The problem is that telling biblical stories is foreign to contemporary experience . . . the assumption is that once you grow up and learn to think you will stop telling stories and start telling the truth." And he adds, "Telling the truth means you will speak in conceptual abstractions."[6]

This was definitely the bias in the homiletics classes I attended in the mid-1970s. I was taught to express ideas propositionally, to use stories as illustrations, yes. However, the stories could not stand alone without some cogent explanation, which in my case usually included a reference to one of my favorite systematic theologians. With the advent of narrative theology and narrative preaching in the past several years, we have seen a paradigmatic shift which is really a return to the oral traditions upon which the scriptures are based. Now, according to William J. Bauch in *Storytelling: Imagination and Faith*, "The tendency is to get closer to the way the raw event was first transmitted: by way of myth, metaphor and story." "This is," he says, "because sooner or later, if we work far enough behind the theology, we're going to get down to the story."[7]

More and more preachers and storytellers, as we enter into this new/old paradigm, are rediscovering the amazing transforming power of stories. Stories like other forms of art can turn our whole world upside down and inside out. Movie director David Hare upon the release of his 1988 film *Paris By Night* said, "People walk around thinking they know what they believe about things, but . . . they rarely examine the reasons for their beliefs . . . when they are confronted with a real work of art then they discover that they don't believe what they thought they believed all along."[8]

Stories not only have transforming power, they are empowering; they transmit real power to the hearer. Consider the scriptural accounts of Jesus' temptations in the wilderness as recorded in Luke 4:1-13 and Matthew 4:1-11. They are based on a personal story, one the church has been remembering and pondering for a long time. It is perhaps the best example we have of the master storyteller telling his own story, although it is not one of the stories we usually think of when we sing, "Tell Me The Stories Of Jesus." This story is Jesus' own personal witness. No one else was there. If the devil has a different version to tell, we have yet to hear it.

What we tend to forget is that this personal witness would have been received as a story. There would have been no doubt about Jesus having struggled with these temptations, but it would have been received as the parables were received, as a story which gives the hearer a glimpse of the new age and invites him or her to participate in it.

No one would have asked Jesus, "Did you really see all the kingdoms of the world? Did the devil really set you up on the pinnacle of the temple? How did you get all the way from the wilderness to the temple? Did you fly through the air; did it happen magically in an instant? No one would have asked him if he really saw the devil, or to describe what the devil looked like. The truth of the story belies the asking of these kinds of questions, and therein lies its marvelous transforming empowerment.

The story is a real manifestation of the power of God. The story doesn't just tell about the power of God's word; there is power in the story. When we hear Jesus quoting scripture in response to the devil's testing, we not only understand its meaning, we feel its strength and force.

It is written, you shall worship the Lord your God and him only shall you serve.

(Luke 4:8)

When I hear that word in the context of the story, I feel its power and I understand how Jesus was able to overcome temptation and accept his calling. But more importantly I am empowered to overcome my temptations and accept my calling too.

Stories are for Everyone

Stories invite the active participation of persons of all ages. Whether told during a sermon or as part of a children's moment, a carefully constructed and well told story can catch the imagination of both young and old, sometimes for different reasons.

"Old Farmer" is a story I told as the conclusion to a sermon on salvation. It has become a favorite of many adults in the churches I have served, but it is also a favorite among the children. "The Little Boy Who Couldn't Sit Still in Church" was told during a children's moment, but was talked about and retold by adults for many weeks afterwards. It was also the occasion for the highest compliment I have ever received after leading in a worship service. An eight-year-old child came up to me, shook my hand, and thanked me for telling it.

For me, stories are by far the best format to use during a children's moment in worship. Stories help to avoid the pitfalls of object lessons and dialogue sermons. There is no temptation to manipulate the children for a cute response in order to get a laugh from the rest of the congregation. Children are not inclined to perform while listening to a story, parents are

12

not as apt to be embarrassed by what their children do or say, everyone is paying attention to the story and not to whatever happens to be the clever object of the day; and most importantly, a story can carry meaning for everyone. Worship does not stop for adults when a story is being told as it sometimes does with other kinds of children's sermons. Instead of becoming spectators or passive observers while children have their time, adults and youth will almost always become active participants as they overhear the story which is told to the children. That is to say, they will be involved in the same way as when a family brings a child forward for baptism or when the choir stands up to sing. They will be able to affirm in their hearts that what is occuring before them is of vital importance to everyone, and something which calls for the very best which they have to give.

In like manner, the word proclaimed from the pulpit, which is usually addressed primarily to the concerns and needs of adults, can also be appealing and meaningful to children when given in the form of a story. It is not necessary for them to understand all of the words or ideas. They will listen in the same way they overhear other adult conversations, thinking about and reflecting on that which is of interest to them and ignoring the rest.

How and When I Tell Stories

It is okay to read a story on some occasions, but it is always better to tell a story. A story told has more power, will catch the imagination more quickly and will hold the attention of the audience longer than a story read. It is not necessary to memorize a story in order to tell it effectively. As Michael Williams teaches in his storytelling seminars, "Pay attention to the setting, characters, objects and actions." It is sometimes helpful to memorize key phrases such as opening lines and dialogue which are essential to the plot, and to key transitions. But in most cases it is best to let the story flow

13

in a conversational way, as one does when telling the events of the day around the supper table.

One of Garrison Keillor's great gifts is his stream of consciousness method of telling. He closes his eyes and pours out a tale from the depths of his memory and imagination, transporting the hearer to the world he creates breath by breath. There is almost a melding of consciousness as one follows his voice to the story's natural and inevitable end.

I am not suggesting that any of us try to imitate Keillor's method or style. We must all find our own storytelling voices which will usually be similar to the way we tell stories in everyday conversation.

I do not tell a story in every sermon. In fact, I tell stories in only about four out of ten sermons. Usually these are occasions on which I cannot say what I want to say, or what I think needs to be said, in any other way. The story "A Corn Fed Beef" came out of my struggle with a text on reconciliation. I needed a conclusion to the sermon that would help the congregation both recognize the need for reconciliation and move toward seeking it with those from whom they were estranged. I could not think of an idea or find an illustration that seemed to work. The story came to me while I was jogging very early on the Sunday morning that I was to preach — just in time.

"The Comforting Word" is a story I wrote after the suicide of a family member. Hearing the scriptures read at his funeral was a great comfort to me. Knowing that there are many in my congregation who have mourned loved ones in similar circumstances, and some who have contemplated suicide themselves, I decided to preach a sermon on the subject. I wanted it to be more than a presentation of, and commentary on, what is said in scripture, though I did do that in the beginning of the sermon. I wanted to share something that would help the congregation to experience the saving, healing, redeeming comfort of God's word. And so I decided to create and tell a story.

14

I tell stories most often at the conclusion of a sermon. Sometimes I will let a story stand alone as a complete story sermon. Once in a while I will tell a story as an introduction to a sermon, and sometimes I will tell one somewhere in the middle, but usually I let the final word of the day be heard in the story. The transitional words for me are "I want to leave you with a story." Often, but not always, I will move from the pulpit to the center of the chancel, tell the story and then, following the example of Fred Craddock, a storytelling preacher I look up to and admire, I turn around and sit down. I give no explanation, nor do I seek in any other way to drive home a point. I don't even say, "Amen". I simply offer the story and leave it as a gift.

These Stories are for You

To all who are touched or in some way renewed by these stories, I give you permission to tell them as your own. You also have my permission to adapt the stories to meet the needs of your particular ministry, as long as the basic integrity of the stories is not compromised. The names, the sex and sometimes the age of characters can be changed without altering the meaning of the story. Settings can also be adjusted in some instances. When telling the story of "The Little Boy Who Couldn't Sit Still In Church," instead of having him count tiles on the ceiling over the pulpit, you may want to have him count whatever it is in your church sanctuary which is obviously countable. When the story is over you can be sure that this part of the story will be remembered, and that the children (and probably the adults, too) will count whatever it is you had the little boy count in the story.

It is my hope that these stories will help persons of all ages to experience the Gospel, and be transformed by it, in the same way that people were transformed when they heard the parables of the master storyteller himself.

The Hardened Heart

*O Lord why dost thou make us err from thy ways
and harden our heart, so that we fear thee not.*
Isaiah 63:17

There was a time when folks said of Henry Jacob, "He
is a hard man. You can see it in his face and in his eyes, especially in his eyes," they said. "He looks at you, but he doesn't
see you."

It all began, this hardness in Henry's heart, just after his
mother died. Henry had just turned thirty. He had never lived
alone before. He had always been a quiet one, but now he became morose and antisocial. He kept to himself. He no longer
returned visits with the neighbors, he stopped going to church;
he hardly left the farm except when he had to go into town
to get supplies. Even then he never said more than was necessary to conduct his business. People got used to it in time. They
stopped asking how he was and after a few cool greetings they
stopped going by the house to see after him.

That's how it was with Henry until he met Grace John-
son. When Henry married Grace he became a different person. Folks said his countenance changed. They called him Hank
now. They said you never saw Hank without a smile on his
face and a twinkle in his eyes. The love of Grace had been
able to penetrate the hardness in Hank's heart allowing the
tender, soft, caring side of his nature to burst forth. He became a pillar in the church and a leader in the community,
known to everyone as a thoughtful, wise and considerate man,
the very opposite of what he had been before.

Grace and Hank settled down on the farm and in time
Grace gave birth to a daughter whom they called Naomi. They
showered her with love and affection all of the days of her

growing and rejoiced and gave thanks to God when the day came for her to marry and go off with her husband to raise a family of her own.

Hank and Grace grew old blissfully together. They became even more active in their church work, they traveled, they went to dances, they tended the flowers in their garden, they spoiled their grandchildren, they enjoyed the company of their friends and they cherished each other. You hardly saw one without the other.

Then Grace died. Hank was devastated. "I might as well be dead too," he said. "I don't think I can live without Grace." He was lost without her and inconsolable. Everyone was afraid he would become hard again. He went to the cemetery every day and talked to Grace. And then one sunny afternoon, exactly three months to the day after Grace's death he bid her farewell, went home and phoned their mutual friend Ruth Joyner.

"Ruth," he said, "I'd like to take you out to supper tonight. What do you say? Shall I pick you up at six?"

Ruth didn't know what to say. Finally she blurted out, "Don't you think it's a little bit too soon, Hank?"

But Hank had made up his mind, so he went straight to the point. "Grace always said, 'Hank, if I die before you do, I want you to promise me that you won't wallow in your grief again. I want you to go out and find someone to share your life with you.' I never promised her," Hank said, "because I couldn't bring myself to consider the possibility. But now I know that she was right. I am not one to live alone." "But," he went on, changing the tone of his voice, "I'm not asking you to marry me, I'm only asking you out to supper. What's wrong with two old friends having supper together?"

Ruth couldn't think of any kind way to say no, so they had supper together. When Hank took her home they sat on her front porch and talked until the last light had been turned out in all the other houses in the neighborhood. After that they were together every day and had supper together every night. For both Hank and Ruth life was sweet again and they were eager to share their joy.

When Hank broke the news about Ruth to Naomi, she was horrified. "Daddy, it's only been three months. How could you do this to Mama? What will people think?" Hank tried to explain it to her but she wouldn't listen to anything he said. Ruth talked to her, too. She tried everything she could think of to make friends with Naomi, but she would have nothing to do with her.

When Christmas came Naomi invited Hank to dinner, but she made it very clear that Ruth was not welcome. Hank wouldn't go without Ruth. He begged Naomi to try to accept Ruth, but she would not relent. From that point on their relationship was strained and a hardness came over Naomi which was to last as long as she lived. Folks said you could see it in her face and in her eyes, especially in her eyes.

Old Farmer

---

*But according to his promise we wait for new
heavens and a new earth in which righteousness
dwells. Therefore, beloved since you wait for these
be zealous to be found by him without spot or blemish, and at peace. And count the forbearance of our
Lord as salvation.*

2 Peter 3:13-15a

In the hills of Southwest Wisconsin, in the little community of Willow Bluff, they tell this story about an old farmer
by the name of Alfie Georgeson. I say old farmer because that's
what everyone called him, "Old Farmer."

The nickname originated one day during a bull session
down at the filling station. It was what one might call a community christening. Some of the guys from the cheese factory
were sitting around the cooler having a pop after work. Alfie
walked in looking like he always looked when he came into
town. Junior Ridley took one look at him and said, "Alfie,
you look like the original old farmer."

It was true. Alfie was never seen wearing anything but the
uniform of his chosen profession, bib overalls. He had three
pairs; one good striped pair which he wore only when he went
into town, and two faded blue pairs which he wore for everyday. One was for wearing while the other was in the wash.
The rest of the uniform was standard issue at any farm supply store; a blue cotton work shirt, triple hook work boots
and Co-op hat. That was Old Farmer.

The name stuck. After a while people began to say it to
his face. "Hey, Old Farmer, how are you doing?" Alfie didn't
mind. That's how he thought of himself, too.

Alfie loved the land. He owned eighty acres of bottom land,
all tillable, which he farmed with a pair of Percheron horses.

Alfie said they were the best work horses in the county, and there wasn't anyone around who would dispute it. Everybody else farmed with tractors. If they had work horses they were only for show or maybe for pulling at the county fair.

Alfie's horses were for working. They had been pulling together for twenty years. They were like old friends. It wasn't that he was against motor propelled machinery. He just never saw the need for it. The farm was paid for, it provided him and Elizabeth with a modest, but adequate, living, and the horses were able to do all of the pulling work that needed to be done. The rest Alfie did by hand. He preferred it that way.

Long days were a way of life on the farm. Alfie's alarm clock went off precisely at 4:30 every morning. He went straight to the barn, fed and watered the livestock, cleaned the stalls, harnessed the horses, spread the manure, fed the chickens and gathered the eggs. He was usually back at the house for breakfast by 7:00, and off to the fields by 7:30.

Field work was done at the horses' pace. When they tired, Alfie rested with them until they were ready to pull again. The end of the day came when the horses had had enough. Alfie never pushed them beyond their endurance, even when he was in a hurry to get something done. There would always be another day. They were usually back in the barn by five, five-thirty at the latest.

The unharnessing was Alfie's favorite part of the day. The ritual had an almost sacramental quality for him. The horses always appreciated the rub down, something they communicated to him in subtle ways that only an old farmer would understand. This and the warm aromas that filled the stalls, a combination of lathered leather, fresh hay, oats in the manger and the pungent odor of the remains of same in the gutter under each horse's tail, made him feel that all was right with the world.

Elizabeth never got used to the fact that be brought these smells with him when he came into the house, although after sixty years she had learned to accept it as one of the givens

20

of farm life. She had been a city girl, if you can call a town of sixteen hundred a city, the daughter of the banker no less. Alfie always said she'd never done a lick of work in her life till she came to the farm. It wasn't true, of course, but Alfie liked to tease her about it just the same. Elizabeth loved Alfie. "My dear old farmer," she used to say when she talked about him with her close friends. She would have been perfectly content only if he would have gone to church with her once in a while. Once or twice a year would have been enough, but he would never go.

It wasn't that Alfie didn't love God. Elizabeth knew that his communication with the Creator was continual. It was part of the rhythm of his life, not in any formal way, of course; they never said grace before meals except on a few occasions when a preacher came to visit; but she knew that God was always in his thoughts as he worked the land. He said so once and she knew it was so because she could see it in his face as she watched him work. It was probably just that he didn't like crowds. Alfie didn't feel comfortable when there were a lot of people around, so he never went anywhere there was going to be a crowd.

He could have liked to have gone for Elizabeth's sake, had almost brought himself to do it on several occasions, but after all those years of not going, it would have been an event. He didn't think he could take all the smiles and self-satisfied looks as people congratulated him and patted him on the back. He knew what they would be thinking. "It's good to see you in church, you old goat! It's about time. Where have you been all of these years?" So he could never bring himself to go, even for Elizabeth's sake. It was a weakness, he knew, but he had never been able to overcome it.

There had been only one exception to this long standing rule and Elizabeth never forgot it. It happened on a Christmas Eve. Elizabeth sang in the choir and when she looked out that particular night just as the service was about to begin she couldn't believe her eyes. There was Alfie sitting in the back row of their little church with the five Enderman kids. He had

21

on his good striped overalls and he looked terribly uncomfortable, but there he was.

Elizabeth found out later why he was there. He told her the kids brought him, but it had been the other way around. The Enderman family lived about a quarter of a mile up the road. They were only there for about a year. Their dad drank and could never hold a job for long, so the family moved around from one run-down farm house to another. But while they were there, the kids came over regularly to see Alfie and Elizabeth. They would talk to Alfie while he worked in the barn and sometimes he would give them a ride in the haywagon. Then they would all go up to the house and Elizabeth would get out the milk and cookies.

That Christmas Eve Elizabeth left early to rehearse with the choir before the service. When the kids came over, Alfie discovered that they knew very little about Christmas. They didn't have a Christmas tree; they didn't expect many presents, and they knew nothing about the birth of Jesus. It didn't seem right to Alfie that any child should grow up without hearing the Christmas story. So he hitched up the horses (Elizabeth had the car), threw some blankets and hay in the back of the wagon, packed the kids in and brought them to church.

Elizabeth learned all of this when they took a tree and the presents over to their house the next day.

After that, Elizabeth picked up the Enderman kids and took them to church every Sunday. She even got their Mom to go once in a while. But once had been enough for Alfie. He never went back.

On Sunday mornings while Elizabeth was in church Alfie would curry the horses and catch up on little odd jobs around the barn. He spent most of his leisure time in the barn. That was just where he wanted to be. And that was where Elizabeth found him that Sunday morning after church. She went to the house first, as she always did, and she didn't go to look for him until long after lunch was ready and she realized he hadn't come in to wash up at the usual time. She found him propped up against a bale of hay. He looked like he always looked when he fell asleep in the easy chair after supper. The doctor told her later that his heart just gave out, said he was surprised that he was able to go on as long as he had.

The church was full on the day of the funeral. Everybody loved "Old Farmer". Elizabeth didn't remember much of what was said. She did remember the fuss everyone made about the horses. She saw to it that Alfie's casket was placed on a hay wagon and drawn to the cemetery by his beloved Percherons. Everybody said it was just the right touch.

And she remembered the preacher reading the familiar words from John:

> *In my Father's house are many rooms; if it were not so, would I have told you that I go now to prepare a place for you? And when I go and prepare a place for you, I will come again and take you to myself, that where I am you may be also. And you know the way where I am going.*

> (John 14:2-4)

She repeated the words in her mind over and over again as she tried in vain to go to sleep that night. Did Alfie know the way? Could Christ in his infinite mercy make a place for him, too?

Author's Note: *"Old Farmer" is dedicated to my father, Alvin Leonard Sumwalt, and in memory of Frank Brown, two old farmers who were part of the inspiration for the story.*

The Little Girl Who
Didn't Like Christmas Presents

. . . the Lord has anointed me to bring good tidings to the afflicted; he has sent me to bind up the brokenhearted, to proclaim liberty to the captives, and the opening of the prison to those who are bound . . .

Isaiah 61:1b

Once upon a time there was a little girl who didn't like to get Christmas presents. Her name was Marcie. Every year when it came time to open the presents under the Christmas tree, Marcie would go to her room and stay there until all of the presents were unwrapped and put away.

One year for Christmas Santa Claus brought Marcie a doll buggy and a baby doll that said, "I love you," when you squeezed it. It was a wonderful gift, but of course Marcie didn't want it. She wouldn't even pick it up. She just went to her room and left the poor baby doll lying all alone under the tree.

Everyone in Marcie's family was getting pretty tired of her attitude toward presents. So finally, on Christmas Day after dinner, her grandmother took her aside for a heart to heart talk. She said, "Marcie, come here and sit on my lap." Marcie's grandmother had a big comfortable lap. "Now Marcie," she said, "tell me why you don't like to get presents."

Marcie didn't say anything at first. She just snuggled in close to her grandmother until she was warm and cozy. Then she said, "Because I'm not good enough."

Marcie's grandmother was surprised. "What ever made you think a thing like that?"

"Well," Marcie said, "people are always telling me to be good so that Santa Claus will come. And you know Grandma, as hard as I try, I can't always be good. So I don't deserve any presents."

Marcie's grandmother smiled and gave her a big hug. And then she told her something that Marcie would never forget. "Marcie, people don't give you presents because you've been good. They give you presents because they love you. We all love you, Marcie, and we would give you presents no matter how good or bad you might have been."

Marcie smiled and gave her grandmother a big kiss. Then she climbed down from her grandmother's comfortable lap, went straight to the Christmas tree, picked up her baby doll and gave it a squeeze. And do you know what the baby doll said?

Christmas Trouble

In the sixth month the angel Gabriel was sent from God to a city of Galilee named Nazareth, to a virgin betrothed to a man whose name was Joseph, of the house of David; and the virgin's name was Mary. And he came to her and said, "Hail, O favored one, the Lord is with you!" But she was greatly troubled at the saying, and considered in her mind what sort of greeting this might be.

Luke 1:26-29

One December evening a group of college students was gathered in the living room of a tiny apartment where their advisor lived, drinking hot chocolate and basking in the afterglow of a caroling experience they had shared at a local nursing home. It was the campus Christian fellowship group led by Professor Joshua Josephson. The students called him Professor Josh for short. He taught physics and chemistry, and because the college was too small to have a chaplain or a chapel, he had started a Bible study group which met every Friday night in the basement of one of the dormitories.

Every year Professor Josh took the group caroling and afterwards he invited them back to his apartment for hot chocolate and giant pop corn balls made from a family recipe which he claimed had been handed down for several generations. This year, as it usually did, the conversation got around to the meaning of Christmas. Stories were told of Christmases past, of presents given and presents received, of family gatherings and candlelight services. Everyone had something to tell about the Christmas pageant in their home church and the parts they had played as children.

After a while Professor Josh broke into the conversation and said, "I have a Christmas story I would like to share with all of you."

"In the little country church where I grew up," he began, "we had a tradition of Christmas caroling in the homes of all the older persons who were unable to come to church. The tradition was started when Miss Bower and Miss Dickenson were our pastors. I never knew their first names. People always referred to them as Miss Bower and Miss Dickenson. They were a tandem. For some reason the bishop always appointed them to serve together and that's the way people always spoke of them. It was impossible to think of one without the other. They shared all of the pastoral duties. One preached one Sunday, the other the next. One was in charge of the Sunday School and the Youth Fellowship group, the other met with the Women's group and the Men's Brotherhood. They used to say that Miss Bower was the best dart ball player the Brotherhood ever had.

"It was Miss Dickenson who organized the caroling expeditions. Miss Bower stayed behind to prepare cookies and hot beverages for the party they always had afterwards at the parsonage.

"The incident I am going to tell you about occurred before I was born. In those days most of the farmers in that part of the country still farmed with horses. When it came time for caroling, they would get out the bobsleds and sleighs which had been stored away all year in the backs of machine sheds and barns. They would pack about a dozen people into each sled, about half as many into each sleigh, and cover everyone with lap robes and horse blankets. Then they would bring out heated soap stones and tuck them down into the straw in the bottom of the rigs to keep their feet warm.

"There is nothing like a sleigh ride in the country with bells ringing and snow glistening on a moonlit night. Sometimes they would pull right up to the windows and sing without getting unbundled. At other places people would insist that everyone come inside so they could see their faces and feed them cookies

27

while they warmed themselves around the stove. The old people looked forward to their coming. For some who couldn't get out at all and who had no family to come to them, it was the only taste of Christmas they would get. There were always a lot of tears and hugs as the last of "Silent Night" was sung and the last "Merry Christmases" were said.

"There was one place where the carolers never received a warm welcome. Old Mrs. Higgens lived all alone in a big farmhouse up at the end of Wheat Hollow. It was the farthest place out on the caroler's route, almost six miles from the church. Mrs. Higgens had been a widow for years. Her children and grandchildren all lived in distant cities, so she rarely saw them. In fact she rarely saw anyone. She hired one of the neighbors to do her shopping and as far as anyone knew he was the only one who ever spoke to her. Every year when the carolers turned up the long lane which led to her house, they would see lights in her kitchen window, but by the time they pulled into the yard the house would be dark. Miss Dickenson always insisted that they sing a few carols anyway but every year there was no response. The house always remained dark.

"One year just before caroling time Miss Dickenson went out to see Mrs. Higgens. Mrs. Higgens must have known who she was. Perhaps she had been expecting her? For whatever reason, she let her in. She took her directly into the parlor, invited her to sit on the davenport, sat herself down on the matching chair, folded her hands in her lap and said, 'Reverend, I'm so glad you've come. I've been wanting to ask you to pray for me.'

" 'Oh,' said Miss Dickenson, 'what would you like me to pray about?'

" 'Well,' said Mrs. Higgens, 'I would like you to ask God to forgive me. I can't find the words to say it myself.'

" 'For what do you need to be forgiven?'' asked Miss Dickenson.

"At this point Mrs. Higgens broke down and the tears flowed for quite a while. 'It's a long story,' she said. 'Years ago before we moved here and before my husband and I were married, we found out that I was expecting. We were engaged to be married, but we were waiting for him to graduate from high school and get a job so he could support us. When we learned about the baby we were beside ourselves. We didn't know what to do. Well, before we could do anything or tell anyone, we were in an accident. We went caroling with a group of kids from the church. One of the horses bolted. The sleigh in which we were riding over-turned and everyone was thrown into the ditch. No one was seriously injured but it was quite a jolt and that night I lost the baby. Somehow, I don't know how, we managed to keep it from our folks. They never found out. The next year Frank and I were married as planned and we moved here to this community partly to get away from the memory of all that. We figured it would be a fresh start for both of us. When you started to bring the carolers around at Christmas time, it brought back all of those memories. And with Frank gone and me here with no one to talk to, it has become more than I can bear.

" 'I understand,' Miss Dickenson said. Then she invited Mrs. Higgens to kneel down with her and they prayed together.

"Not long after that, late one Sunday evening, Miss Bower and Miss Dickenson heard a knock on their parsonage door. When they opened the door, they were surprised to see that it was a girl named Mary from the Youth Fellowship group. She said she had to talk to someone. Miss Dickenson took her into the study, and before she could take her coat or offer her a chair, Mary blurted out that she was pregnant. She said she knew better and they hadn't intended for it to happen, but it had happened and now what was she going to do? She said she was afraid to tell her folks and she didn't know if her boyfriend would marry her. She wasn't sure if she wanted to get married. She had almost a year of school left and where would they live? How could they afford to take care of a baby?

"Miss Dickenson listened and when Mary was finished she said the usual things that pastors say to young girls who come to them in that kind of trouble. But Mary was not to be comforted. It was as if she hadn't heard a word Miss Dickenson

29

said. Finally, almost in desperation Miss Dickenson told her, 'You must tell your folks. I'll go with you if you like. But before you tell them, I want you to pay a visit to old Mrs. Higgens.'

"If she hadn't had Mary's attention before, she had it now. 'Old Mrs. Higgens?' she said. 'Why in the world would you want me to go and see her? Besides she won't see me, she won't see anyone.'

" 'Yes, she will,' Miss Dickenson said, 'I'll arrange it.'

"The next day after school Mary drove up Wheat Hollow to see old Mrs. Higgens. She didn't know why she was going, but she had told Miss Dickenson she would go, so she went. When she got to the door Mrs. Higgens was waiting for her. She said, 'Hello Mary,' and then she ushered her directly into the parlor. She sat her down on the davenport, sat herself down beside her and before Mary could say a word, she poured out her whole story just the way she had told it to Miss Dickenson. And then she added one more thing. She looked Mary straight in the eye and said, 'My baby would have been sixty-two years old this year.'

"By this time, of course, Mary was crying. Through her tears she thanked Mrs. Higgens and told her she knew now what she had to do.

"That year when the Christmas carolers drove up Wheat Hollow to Mrs. Higgens' place she left the lights on. And when they got to the door she invited them in and insisted that they stay for hot chocolate and cookies."

And then Professor Josh paused for a moment before he said, "Mary Josephson is my mother. She never married my father, but she loved me and raised me as if I were God's own beloved son."

Author's Note: *"Christmas Trouble"* is dedicated in memory of Miss Sarah Mauer and Miss Matie Richardson who were the pastors of the Loyd and Ithaca Evangelical United Brethren Churches at the time when I was baptized in the early 1950s. The story is fiction. I share it as a gift for that is how it came to me, as a gift of the Spirit. It is also my tribute to Miss Mauer and Miss Richardson whose shared ministry was a blessing to so many and for whose witness I shall always be grateful.

Bleak Midwinter:
An R-Rated Christmas Story

And the angel said to them, "Be not afraid; for behold I bring you good news of a great joy which will come to all the people; for to you is born this day in the city of David a savior, who is Christ the Lord. And this will be a sign for you: you will find a babe wrapped in swaddling cloths and lying in a manger." And suddenly there was with the angel a multitude of the heavenly host praising God and saying, "Glory to God in the highest, on earth peace among men with whom he is pleased."

Luke 2:10-14

Then Herod when he saw that he had been tricked by the wisemen, was in a furious rage, and he sent and killed all the male children in Bethlehem and in all that region who were two years old or younger . . .

Matthew 2:16

Mid-December. Snow fell lightly outside a big farmhouse covering the fields around with a cool white blanket which would keep the fragile alfalfa roots safe until spring. Inside happy voices could be heard laughing and singing over the soft twinkle of Elsie Barnett's baby grand piano, the one Herb had bought for her to replace her old upright. Herb was gone now, dead almost two years. They had used his memorial money to buy a second baby grand for the church for Elsie to play in worship. The two pianos had become Elsie's source of life. Music was her salvation. It gave her an important function in the church and community. How she loved to play and sing!

31

Byron Bain parked his pickup truck near the other vehicles next to the barn and made his way slowly, somewhat uncertainly, toward the light and warmth of the house. He could hear the music, the sweet blend of Elsie's playing and the voices of her guests floating out over the snow. It was to him like the tantalizing aroma of food cooking before a meal. It touched something deep inside of him, a hunger for acceptance, for physical comfort and love. The sound heightened his anticipation for the evening of fellowship to which he had been invited. And it whetted the ache of longing which had permeated his being for so many years. Perhaps there was hope. Perhaps tonight he would be able to tell her.

Byron loved Elsie, always had, for as long as he could remember. They had been in grade school together — and he had neighbored with her and Herb for nearly forty years. He had never been able to tell her, had been too timid to tell her before she fell in love with Herb, hadn't even dared to consider the possibility as long as Herb was alive — but now it was just a matter of waiting for the right moment. He stopped by regularly to give a hand with minor repairs and other little things she wasn't able to do for herself. Sometimes Elsie would offer him a cup of coffee and they would sit and talk.

He glanced through the window into the living room as he climbed up the steps onto the porch. Martin Van Able was there, the widower from up the road, standing next to the piano looking over Elsie's right shoulder. The McCallums, Lucy and Burt who used to live on the old Stringer place but had retired the year before last and moved into town, were sitting on the couch. Jim, Elsie's son, and his wife, Janet, were in the love seat at the far end of the room. The twins, Heather and Holly, they were about eleven now, were sitting on the bench on either side of their grandmother. And their brother little Jimmy, Jim and Janet's youngest and thus still called "little" though he was bigger than most other nine year olds, was standing on the other side of Elsie across from Martin, looking over her other shoulder.

32

"Let's sing my favorite carol," Byron heard Elsie call out. Her voice was only slightly muffled by the pane of glass that separated him from the living room. Elsie launched into "O Little Town of Bethlehem" as Byron crossed the porch and opened the door into the front hall. The sound of the voices swelled now filling the whole house, the familiar words about that faraway place and time seemed to lift them beyond the moment into some timeless, non-material dimension.

> . . . *how still we see thee lie*
> *above thy deep and dreamless sleep*
> *the silent stars go by*
> *yet in the dark streets shineth*
> *the everlasting light*
> *the hopes and fears of all the years*
> *are met in thee tonight.*

Byron entered the living room and stood next to the giant Christmas cactus on the oak stand just inside the doorway. It was hanging heavy with pink red buds that looked as if they could burst into full flower at any moment. No one seemed to notice him come in. They were still caught up in the song.

"You girls sing the next verse," Elsie said. There was no doubt that they were her favorites. She had always been close to the twins. Jimmy had his own special place in her heart. He had been Herb's favorite. They had fished and hunted together, but the girls were her girls and that was all there was to it. She had taught them how to sing together and had had them sing often in the worship service at church. Their sweet voices melded together as one in angelic tones reminiscent of those that were heard that night over the shepherd's field.

> . . . *O Holy child of Bethlehem*
> *descend to us we pray*
> *cast out our sin and enter in*
> *be born in us today*[9]

When they had sung all of the verses Elsie gave each of her girls a squeeze, got up from the bench and declared, "Now before we have our ice cream and pie, I have an announcement to make." She stepped over next to Martin Van Able and took hold of his hand. There was a moment of quiet astonishment as Elsie's guests exchanged quizzical glances. No one had expected anything like this. The color drained from Byron's face but no one noticed. Everyone was staring at Elsie.

"I expect this will come as something of a shock to all of you," she began, "but we couldn't wait to tell you. Martin and I are going to be married." She was glowing now. "Sometime next spring," she said. "He asked me last night and I accepted." And then looking at their faces and seeing the amazement that was still in their eyes, she continued somewhat hesitantly, "I hope you will be happy for us." They all moved to embrace them and to speak the obligatory words of congratulations, all except Byron. He walked quietly out of the living room, picked up his coat and left the house without a word.

After the hugs and a few awkward moments of silence as the news of this unexpected union was gradually absorbed into their collective consciousness, Elsie and Martin fielded a host of questions.

"Well, when did all of this come about?"

"How long have you two been conspiring together?"

"Where will you live?"

"What will become of the farm?"

"Who will be in the wedding?" one of the twins wanted to know. They would both be flower girls they were assured and Jimmy was to be the ring bearer.

And after everyone was satisfied that life would go on in an acceptable way, and they had begun to share Elsie and Martin's joy, they all settled down for a winter evening repast.

Elsie went into the kitchen to get the coffee and dessert. Jimmy sneaked out the back door to check on the dogs. Everyone else moved back to their original seats and the conversation gradually returned to the more mundane concerns of crops, weather, the price of corn and the new dog track that had opened up in town. Still no one noticed that Byron was not there.

He was standing down by his pickup truck, staring back at the house. The door to the cab was half open, its interior dimly illuminated by a flickering dome light which was affixed to the center of the roof directly over the gun rack.

"To be so close," Byron thought, "after all these years. I know she loves me. How could she do this to me? What's wrong with me?" He screamed the words in his mind, clenching his fists and grinding his teeth hard together. The sound of laughter poured out from the living room, piercing the cold night air. It seemed to Byron that it grew louder and louder, ringing in his ears again and again. His heart began to pound, his throat tightened, he found it difficult to swallow, his breathing slowed, almost stopped. He gasped for breath. The lights in the house swam before his eyes. Byron thought for a moment that he was going to pass out in the snow. But something inside was driving him to resist — to fight back. All the hurt and anger of a lifetime of failures and disappointments erupted from the nether regions of his soul like molten lava gushing out of a hot volcano. He reached into the cab and took the gun. In one motion he slid the gun from its case, cocked it, turned and moved deliberately toward the house.

The only thing he could remember when they questioned him later was the sound of the gun firing again and again. He would hear the echo of the shots resounding in his memory for as long as he lived. He could almost count them.

"Did I kill them all?" He finally forced himself to ask the question.

Elsie and the little boy were unhurt, they told him. The rest were dead.

Byron wished himself dead. As they put him in a cell and he heard the door close behind him, he wondered why he hadn't ended it for himself as well. Thinking of the pain he had caused Elsie was more than he could bear. There was nothing left for him now. He lay on the cell bed staring into the blackness, silently cursing the whole wasted life he had lived.

35

Near the end of that first long day, Byron was roused from his moribund trance by a flash of light which came through the narrow window over the commode next to the bed. When he stood on top of it, carefully positioning his feet on each side of the opening so as not to slip on the grimy porcelain, he could see a metal cross atop the spire of the church across the street. The cross had caught one of the last starry rays of the setting sun and reflected it mercifully through the window of his cell.

Byron clung to the edge of the window with one hand and with the other he made a fist which he shook furiously in the direction of the cross. "Where were you when I needed you," he shouted, "why didn't you stop me?"

The following week there were three funerals on successive days at the church across the street from the jail. No one noticed Byron's eyes watching from the third floor window as seven caskets passed in and out the great doors of the church. On the last day as the four Barnett caskets were carried away in a parade of gray hearses, Byron looked for the first time since the night of his blind rage upon the faces of Elsie and Jimmy. He was glad that they had been spared and he tried to weep for them but found himself denied even the comfort of tears.

Christmas Eve came too soon that year. A heavy snow fell in big wet flakes from dark December clouds as the reluctant worshipers trudged through the slush, dutifully taking their places in well worn pews. The church was soon full as it had been for each of the funerals the week before and the funeral atmosphere prevailed. There was no joy, no sense of anticipation. They greeted each other with subdued voices, whispering and nodding greetings as they cast furtive glances at the bereaved families who were also present in their usual places. It was almost as if the caskets were still open before them.

They went through the motions of worship, singing without feeling, repeating the prayers without thought. The minister was dreading the sermon. He didn't know what he could say that might penetrate the all-pervasive gloom.

The Christmas anthem came just before the sermon. Elsie was to play. She had insisted on it, said there was no reason to put it off. She had been through this before and besides the music would help. So no one was surprised when she took her usual place at the keyboard in front of the baby grand. There were some murmurs though when Jimmy got up and sat down beside her on the bench. "He's going to turn the pages for her," someone whispered. But Elsie didn't need help with page-turning. Jimmy was there to sing. They sang the first verse together, tentatively in the beginning but then in perfect harmony as the congregation began to resonate with them and the music, the old woman in a trained alto voice well past its prime and the young boy in a pure perfect soprano:

In the bleak midwinter, frosty wind made moan, earth stood hard as iron, water like a stone; snow had fallen, snow on snow, snow on snow, in the bleak midwinter long ago.

Elsie let Jimmy sing out alone on the second verse.

Our God in heaven cannot hold him, nor earth sustain; heaven and earth shall flee away when he comes to reign.

Outside the snow had stopped and the clouds had begun to lift. Across the street Byron Bain stood precariously on his tiptoes atop the commode in his jail cell straining to get a full view of the church. He could hear the music faintly through a crack in the cell window, the heavenly blend of Elsie's playing and the sweet angelic voice of her grandson floating out over the snow. And then his eye was taken by a speck of light twinkling beyond the cross in the Eastern sky, the first evening star, shining ever brighter moment by moment as it rose slowly over the dark world below.

In the bleak midwinter, Jimmy sang, a stable sufficed the Lord God Almighty, Jesus Christ.[10]

37

Author's Note: *(Verses 16-18 from the second chapter of Matthew are omitted from all three cycles of the Common Lectionary. We don't like to hear about the slaughter of innocents on Christmas Eve. We prefer Luke's more tranquil pastoral scenes. But Herod's rage and the massacre he orders as a result are an important part of the story. Jesus was born into the real world after all and it is in this real world of violence and suffering that he does his saving work. The tragic scene described in these three verses stands in stark contrast to the rest of the Christmas story as told by both Luke and Matthew. The congregation will feel the power of this and it will put in their minds the question which the story addresses.)*

This story is appropriate for Christmas Eve in cycles A, B, or C — and can also be told on the first Sunday after Christmas in Cycle C.

A Partial Order of Worship

First Reader	Luke 2:8-14
Duet	"O Little Town of Bethlehem" Verses 1-2
Second Reader	Matthew 2:1-12
Duet	"O Little Town of Bethlehem" Verses 3-4
First Reader	Matthew 2:13-18
Story Teller	"Bleak Midwinter: An R-Rated Christmas Story"
Solo	"In the Bleak Midwinter" Verse 1
Choir	"In the Bleak Midwinter" Verses 2-3
Congregation	"In the Bleak Midwinter" Verse 4
Story Teller	Matthew 2:19-23
Congregation	"O Morning Star, How Fair and Bright"

Christmas in Canaan

When the angels went away from them into heaven,
the shepherds said to one another, "Let us go over
to Bethlehem and see this thing that has happened,
which the Lord has made known to us."

Luke 2:15

Once upon a time on Christmas Eve just before the turn of the century, somewhere on the trail between St. Louis and the Oklahoma Territory, a child was born in a dugout barn with the aid of a blind midwife and an angel of the Lord.

Silas and Millie Kittleson were on their way from Indiana to Oklahoma where they intended to homestead and raise their family. Millie was expecting. It would be their first child. She had celebrated her seventeenth birthday on the day they passed through St. Louis. Silas was a seasoned young man of twenty-three, an experienced horseman and veteran trailblazer. He had made the trip several times before and was confident that they would arrive safely in Nickerson, Kansas, before the baby was due. There they would winter with relatives before going on to Oklahoma in the spring.

It was risky to cross the plains with mules and wagon any time in winter. But it had been a mild December with little snow and wind. The towns were frequent and the dirt roads well worn and marked, so they had just kept pushing on day after day. Nickerson was only about twenty miles away. They would make it in time for Christmas. Silas' aunt and uncle would be delighted.

It was about three o'clock in the afternoon that December twenty-fourth that Millie felt the first contractions. Silas had just guided the mules across a small stream. When they pulled up on the bank they saw what appeared to be farm buildings low against the horizon about a mile-and-a-half in the distance. Perhaps they could get some help and find shelter for the night. But as they drew near they could see that what had once been a prairie homestead was now abandoned and very much in disrepair. There was a small house with a sod roof which had collapsed on one end. About thirty yards from the house was a dugout barn which was still pretty much intact. It was a combination log and sod construction and considerably larger than the house. There was hay in the loft and the faint odor of horses and cattle could be detected in the stalls below.

Silas unharnessed the mules, moved them into the stalls and fed them some of the old musty hay. The mules' body heat would help to warm them through the night. Millie made a bed for herself with blankets and hay in the empty stall across from the mules. The contractions were more frequent now. She called out to Silas, "Come here and hold me. I'm frightened." Silas held her close, trying not to let on how frightened he was feeling himself. Together they prayed to God for the safe delivery of their child.

About an hour later there was a loud banging on the barn door and then a voice. "I heard you folks might be in need of some help." When they opened the door there was an old woman, hunched over and leaning on a cane. She appeared to be in her eighties.

"I'm a midwife," she said. "I deliver the babies around here. I've delivered most all the babies born in Rush County, Kansas for over sixty years. They call me Old Catherine. Don't think I hear 'em. You can call me Kate. That's what my mother called me. I don't see too well anymore. You will have to lead me around a bit. But I know about birthing babies. I've delivered over a hundred in my time and never lost a mother or a baby."

The child was born within the hour. It came breach. Old Catherine said it was a good thing she got there when she did.

And then the neighbors began to come; farmers and ranchers with their wives and children. They brought gifts. The children offered toys, wooden rattles, tops, cornhusk dolls, whistles carved from willow twigs. The women brought more practical things; pillows, blankets, cotton rags, baby clothes, and enough food to feed a thrashing crew. One of the men had fashioned a cradle out of a feed trough. It wasn't until everyone started to leave that Silas thought to ask how it was that they had heard about them.

"Didn't you send her?" It was Old Catherine who spoke first. "She said you needed me and then she rode with me across the prairie. I could never have made it by myself. She was a young woman about twenty years old." Everyone else said they had seen the same woman. "She said come quickly, that a baby was being born out at Canaan."

And then they all knew who it was. There was a moment of utter astonishment and wonder as people exchanged bewildered glances and nods. Old Catherine turned to Silas and Millie and said out loud what everyone was thinking. "There was only one person who ever called this place Canaan. Liza Campbell. Liza and Jed Campbell came here to homestead about twenty years ago. They built the house and barn, and when they were finished Liza said, "We will call it Canaan. It is our very own promised land." They put up a sign right out there by the well. 'Welcome to Canaan' it said."

"What became of them?" Millie asked.

Again it was Old Catherine who spoke. "Liza died in childbirth about a year after they settled here. They sent for me, but she died before I could get here. Jed was heartbroken, went back East. We never heard from him again."

There was a long silence as everyone pondered this strange and marvelous occurrence. Could it have been Liza? Who else could it have been? But why, and how?

Suddenly their ponderings were interrupted by the crying of the newborn child.

They called him Elmer. Elmer Milton, after Millie's father. And for as long as they lived they never ceased giving thanks to God for the mysterious messenger who had announced his birth.

The Day After Christmas

. . . Mary kept all these things, pondering them in her heart.

Luke 2:19b

It was the day after Christmas and Gary felt sad. There was no more excitement in the air. All the presents had been opened, Grandpa and Grandma had gone home, the batteries were just about played out on his new racing set, one of the pedals on his Big Wheel got bent when his sister tried to ride it down the basement stairs, the sweater his aunt Nancy sent him from Montana was too small and there wasn't enough snow on the hill to try out his new sled. But worst of all, next Christmas was a whole year away. It didn't seem fair that Christmas should be over so soon. Why couldn't every day be like Christmas, Gary wondered as he stared at the empty place under the tree where all the presents had been? Somehow a Christmas tree just wasn't the same without presents.

Christmas was Gary's favorite holiday. He had fun on the fourth of July waving sparklers and watching the fireworks, he liked dressing up on Halloween, he enjoyed eating turkey and dressing on Thanksgiving Day, and he delighted in hunting eggs on Easter, but none of these compared with Christmas. There was something special about Christmas. Gary liked shopping for presents at the mall, he liked visiting Santa and sitting on his lap, he liked singing Christmas carols at church and playing a shepherd in the Christmas pageant, he liked going to Mr. and Mrs. Whirry's ranch to cut down the Christmas tree, he liked decorating the tree with lights and tinsel, and he especially liked running down the stairs on Christmas morning to see the tree surrounded with presents of all shapes and sizes. It was fun to try to find all the ones with his name on them and even more fun to try to guess what was in them. But his absolute favorite part of Christmas was when his Mom and Dad came downstairs and his Dad read the story from the Bible, and then they all opened their presents. Gary liked everything about Christmas but he didn't like it when it was over.

That night when Gary's Mom tucked him into bed he asked her why every day couldn't be like Christmas? His Mom smiled and then she said, "Do you remember, in the Christmas story, how exciting it was for Mary and Joseph when the baby Jesus was born, and when the shepherds came and told them about the angel and the singing of the heavenly host? How do you think they felt the next day when all of the excitement was over?"

Gary thought about it for a while and then he said, "I think they must have felt a little sad, but they had the baby Jesus and they knew he was going to grow up to be the savior. I think that must have made them very glad."

Suddenly Gary didn't feel so sad that Christmas was over. He remembered all the wonderful things that had happened on Christmas Day. "It was enough," he thought, "to last him for a long, long time, at least until next Christmas." Then he smiled at his Mom and wished her one last Merry Christmas.

Out of the Water

---

*In those days Jesus came from Nazareth of Galilee
and was baptized by John in the Jordan. And when
he came up out of the water, immediately he saw
the heavens open and the Spirit descending upon him
like a dove; and a voice came from heaven, "Thou
art my beloved son; with thee I am well pleased."*

Mark 1:9-11

Elsie Dewitt was upset when she came into the sanctuary.
She wasn't able to sit in her usual place near the middle of
the pew. The Murphys usually saved it for her, but they were
out of town today, and there were several visitors in their
places. Elsie had to sit near the end of the pew, next to the
center aisle. She didn't like to sit next to the aisle. That was
where her late husband had always sat. But that wasn't the
only reason she was upset. It was the second Sunday of the
month, baptism Sunday. She could see at least three families
with babies sitting near the front, not far from the baptismal
font. No doubt the visitors in her pew were relatives of one
of these families.

Elsie had to force herself to come to church on baptism
Sundays. She came partly because she didn't know how she
could explain to her friends why she didn't want to come, but
mostly because she could never justify not going to worship.
Elsie had been raised to believe that the Lord's day belonged
to God. She always went to worship on Sunday. She wouldn't
miss for any reason. Any other Sunday she would have been
glad to have been there. Worship was a joy for her. Elsie had
never thought of it as a duty. But baptism Sundays were different. They were something she suffered, like one might endure

the occasional migraine headache. She viewed it as part of her lot in life.

The reason was a secret that she had shared with no one, not even her late husband. Her parents had known, of course, but they were long gone.

Midway through the service, Elsie's heart skipped a beat. The pastor was headed her way, carrying one of the babies she had just baptized. It was a custom in the church for the pastor to give each baptized baby to someone in the congregation to hold during the baptismal prayer, as a way of welcoming him or her into the family of God. "It couldn't be. Oh no!" Elsie thought, as the pastor smiled at her and handed her the baby. One of her greatest fears had been realized. Now what was she going to do? She couldn't just hand the baby back to the pastor and ask her to give him to someone else. The child deserved better than that on his important day. But it wasn't right, it just wasn't right. She, who had failed in her duty to her own child, had no business holding the child of another during the consummation of a sacrament.

Elsie bit her lip and hung on to the baby, trying hard not to let her discomfort show. She breathed a sigh of relief when, at last, the pastor finished the prayer and took the baby back to his parents. The worst was over. But how could she ever forgive herself for allowing it to happen? Elsie waited in agony for the next standing hymn. Then she got up quietly and left the church.

That afternoon Elsie called the pastor and asked if she could see her at her earliest convenience. She was determined to relieve herself of the burden of the terrible secret she had carried alone for all of these years. Elsie knew that if she didn't share it now, she would carry it with her into eternity.

Pastor Carol agreed to see her at two o'clock the next afternoon. Elsie arrived promptly at the appointed hour. She looked pale, and her eyes were swollen and red. "I couldn't sleep at all last night," she told Pastor Carol. "I've been deeply troubled ever since the baptisms yesterday. You may have noticed that I left the service early."

"I did see you go," Pastor Carol said, "and I'm glad you've come to talk about it."

"I'll have to start at the very beginning," Elsie said. And then she poured it all out. "I had a child out of wedlock when I was sixteen. My folks kept me home from school as soon as they found out I was expecting. Dad simply told the teacher that I was needed on the farm. In those days that was a common occurrence, so no one thought anything about it. And no one ever found out about the baby. My mother assisted me in the delivery. That went well enough, but the baby was small, and he had difficulty breathing from the first day. I knew I should have sent for the pastor and had him baptized, but I was afraid of what he might say. So we never sent for him. The baby died two weeks after he was born. We buried him in the family cemetery on the ridge behind the house. I told my husband about the baby before we were married, but I have never been able to tell anyone about my failure to have him baptized. I tried to put it out of my mind, but every time I see a baby baptized in church, I remember, and I wonder if my baby is all right. I can't imagine that God would keep him out of heaven just because he hadn't been baptized, but I don't know. I worry about it, and even more now that I'm older."

Then Elsie broke down and wept. Pastor Carol got up, put her arms around her, and held her for a long time.

The next Sunday morning after the sermon, Pastor Carol announced that Elsie had something she wanted to share with everyone. Elsie got up from where she was sitting in her usual pew, walked hesitantly all the way up the aisle, then turned and stood facing the congregation about three feet in front of the baptismal font. Pastor Carol handed her the microphone. Elsie took a deep breath, and then she told them the whole story, just as she had related it in the pastor's office. When she was finished Pastor Carol took the cover off the baptismal font and invited everyone in the congregation to join hands as they prayed. And then, calling Elsie's long lost child by name, she commended him to God. Then she prayed the Prayer of Thanksgiving Over the Water:

Pour out your Holy Spirit,
to bless this gift of water
and those who receive it,
to wash away their sin
and clothe them in righteousness
throughout their lives,
that dying and being raised
with Christ, they may share
in his final victory.[11]

When the prayer was finished, Pastor Carol invited the congregation to come forward and dip their hands into the water and remember their baptisms. They all came. Elsie was the last to come. Her hands trembled as she lifted them up out of the water. Somewhere from deep inside herself she heard a voice saying that all was well.

Author's Note: *The complete Prayer of Thanksgiving Over the Water can be found on pages 41 and 42 of The United Methodist Hymnal.*

The Little Boy
Who Couldn't Sit Still in Church

O God, thou art my God, I seek thee, my soul thirsts for thee; my flesh faints for thee, as in a dry and weary land where no water is. So I have looked upon thee in the sanctuary, beholding thy power and glory. Because thy steadfast love is better than life, my lips will praise thee. So I will bless thee as long as I live; I will lift up my hands and call on thy name.

Psalm 63:1-4

Once upon a time there was a little boy who couldn't sit still in church. His Mom and Dad were very unhappy with him. The people sitting in front and behind were always frowning at him, and he was sure from the stern looks the pastor gave him that she didn't like him very much either.

One Sunday morning during the singing of the second hymn his Dad motioned for him to get up and follow him. He took him by the arm and led him out of the sanctuary, through the narthex and up the stairs to the balcony. The little boy didn't know what to expect, but he knew from the way his Dad was holding onto his arm that it wasn't going to be good.

His Dad took him to the very last pew in the top row of the balcony. He sat him down and then he said, "Now you sit here by yourself until you can learn to sit still in church."

The little boy felt very embarrassed. Everyone had seen his Dad lead him up the aisle and out of the sanctuary. Everyone knew it was because he couldn't sit still. The little boy felt very bad. And he felt even worse when he noticed some of his friends peeking up over the pews to see what had happened to him. He felt bad enough to cry, but he didn't dare cry while his friends were watching. He would have liked to run out to

48

the parking lot to sit in the car, but he knew if he did, things would be a lot worse when his Dad got hold of him later. So, he just sat there with his head in his hands feeling sorry for himself.

After a little while he felt a hand on his shoulder. It was old Mr. Gibbons, the head usher. Mr. Gibbons had been head usher for as long as the little boy could remember. Everyone loved him. He was like a part of the church building. It made you feel good just to see him there every Sunday morning.

Mr. Gibbons came around and sat down next to the little boy. He didn't say anything for a long time, but when he did speak he got right to the point. He said, "Watch closely what everyone else does while they are sitting still in church." This surprised the little boy, and he gave Mr. Gibbons a rather puzzled look. "Just watch," Mr. Gibbons said, "do you see?" The little boy looked and looked, but he couldn't figure out what Mr. Gibbons was talking about.

"Watch their feet and legs," he said. The little boy looked at all of the feet and legs under the pews. Some people had their legs crossed, others had their legs stretched out straight in front of them, and some had both feet planted firmly together beneath the pew.

And then the little boy noticed a curious thing. Every once in a while everything changed. Crossed legs were stretched out straight, stretched legs were crossed or angled in another direction and firmly planted feet were tucked back underneath the pew. All of this occurred very quietly, of course, so that you wouldn't notice unless you happened to be looking.

The little boy turned to Mr. Gibbons and said with some delight in his voice, "I think I see what you mean."

"Now," said Mr. Gibbons, "look at their heads and arms."

The little boy looked. This time he was not surprised at what he saw. Some heads were tilted to the right side, some were tilted to the left; a few were nodding, and one man looked like he was sound asleep. There were arms in many different positions. Some were holding up heads, a few were folded

49

gently on laps and some were stretched out straight across the backs of the pews. Again he noticed that every once in a while there was a complete realignment. Nodding heads became tilted heads, tilted heads nodded or were tilted in another direction. Stretched arms were folded and folded arms were unfolded and refolded in another position. The man who was sleeping woke up and one of the high school girls who had been out late the night before began to nod off.

"You see," said Mr. Gibbons, "no one sits perfectly still in church."

"I never noticed before," said the little boy.

"I know," said Mr. Gibbons. "You were too busy not sitting still. Only you did it in ways that disturbed other people. The trick is to move around very carefully in a way that doesn't bother anyone."

The little boy felt relieved. Not sitting still in church wasn't so bad after all. He just had to learn to do it like everyone else did. He watched very carefully until the service was over.

The next Sunday when they came to church, his Dad warned him that he had better sit still or he would find himself back up in the balcony. The little boy assured him that there would be no need to go through all of that again.

When the service started he took a deep breath and crossed his legs. That lasted through the prelude and the call to worship. Then came the hymn. Hymns were easy because you got to stand up and sing. The little boy liked to sing, so that part was no problem at all.

Following the hymn came the prayer of confession, the scripture reading and the creed. The scripture reading was a little long that day, but by folding and refolding his arms and adjusting the tilt on his head he managed to get safely through to the creed and the Gloria Patri. He liked saying the creed and singing the Gloria because he knew them both by heart.

Everything else went pretty well until it came time for the sermon. He almost lost it during the sermon. Sermons were always the hardest part. They were usually long and mostly about things that were of no interest to him. He caught himself just as he was about to wiggle in a way that had gotten him into trouble so many times before. Instead he quietly crossed his legs, tilted his head upward in the direction of the pulpit and silently counted the tiles in the ceiling over the pastor's head. He was surprised to discover that he could count tiles and listen to the sermon at the same time.

By the time the service was over the little boy was feeling very pleased with himself. No one had frowned at him during the whole service, and his parents did not have to remind him to sit still even once. What's more, he had not only listened to all of the sermon and remembered most of it, he also knew exactly how many tiles there were in the ceiling over the pastor's head. It had been a wonderful Sunday.

After worship the little boy went up to Mr. Gibbons and said, "Mr. Gibbons, I want to thank you for helping me to learn how to sit still in church."

Mr. Gibbons smiled, and then with a twinkle in his eye he said something the little boy would never forget. "You mean you want to thank me for teaching you how to get away with not sitting still in church!"

"That's right," said the little boy, and he laughed with Mr. Gibbons. He knew he would never get into trouble for not sitting still in church again.

Author's Note: *This story is dedicated to Fred Gibson, Larry McGranahan and Walter Larsen, three head ushers I have known who are very much like Mr. Gibbons.*

A Place to Hide

. . . at a time of distress, in the rush of great waters, they shall not reach him. Thou art a hiding place for me, thou preservest me from trouble; thou dost encompass me with deliverance.

Psalm 32:6-7

Benjamin Dalton wanted to hide. He would have crawled under his desk but that was where the problem lay. There was a puddle directly under his seat. No, the roof wasn't leaking and the school plumbing was working fine, but there was a wet streak running all the way up one of his pants legs.

Benjamin didn't know why it had happened. It had never happened before. He made it all the way through kindergarten, first grade and second grade and never had a problem like this. This sort of thing wasn't supposed to happen to third graders. But there it was and Mrs. Butler was headed his way. What was he going to do?

He was sure everyone would laugh and make fun of him. He would be the laughing stock of the whole school. All of the big boys would tease him and the girls would probably never speak to him again.

Benjamin couldn't remember ever being in a worse situation in his life. He had wet the bed at home a few times and his parents had always been very understanding. But this was school!

How was it the Sunday School teacher said you were supposed to pray when you were in trouble?

Just then Alicia Gordon walked by. She had been to the sink to put fresh water in the fish bowl. She was trying to walk very carefully so as not to spill any water while returning it to the window sill.

52

Suddenly Alicia tripped. No one stuck out a foot and there was nothing in the aisle; she just tripped. The fish bowl went flying through the air and landed upside down in Benjamin's lap. Water poured all over his pants and spilled onto the floor under his desk. One of the goldfish ended up in his shirt pocket and the other one went sliding across the room toward Mary Lou Felton's desk.

Benjamin's pants were soaked and there was water everywhere. He couldn't believe his good fortune. He was saved. Now no one would ever know about his embarrassing accident. He pretended to be upset with Alicia when Mrs. Butler came to clean up the mess. But it was all he could do to keep from hugging her.

Somehow Benjamin managed to get through the rest of the school day. Mrs. Butler found him an old pair of gym shorts to wear while his pants dried in the furnace room. He enjoyed the extra attention he got from all the kids who felt sorry for him because he got all wet. And he felt sorry for Alicia because everyone was teasing her for being such a klutz. What a strange turn of events.

While he was waiting for the bus, Benjamin noticed Alicia standing all alone, so he went over to talk to her. He didn't know what made him say it, he just seemed to blurt it out. "You tripped on purpose, didn't you, Alicia?"

Alicia just smiled. Then she said, "I wet the bed once when I was staying overnight with my aunt and uncle in St. Louis. I remembered how awful I felt when they found out."

Benjamin squeezed her hand quickly so no one could see. He saw her smile as he ran to get on the bus.

On the way home Benjamin said a prayer, thanking God for Alicia Gordon.

The Woman Who Felt Small

Bless the Lord, O my soul; and all that is in me, bless his holy name! Bless the Lord, O my soul, and forget not his benefits, who forgives all your iniquity, who heals all your diseases, who redeems your life from the pit, who crowns you with steadfast love and mercy, who satisfies you with good as long as you live so that your youth is renewed like the eagle's.

Psalm 103:1-5

There was once a tiny old woman who lived in a nursing home in a small county seat town. Her name was Margaret Trotter. Everyone called her Maggie for short.

Whenever anyone asked Margaret how she was, she would reply in a very dignified voice, "I feel small." It wasn't just that she was tiny, although she weighed only eighty-three pounds and she stood less than five feet tall. It was that, as she said, she felt small.

Margaret had been small all of her life. They used to call her "Tiny" when she was in grade school. "Here comes teeny tiny Maggie," the children would cry. At first the teasing bothered Margaret but after awhile she decided to ignore it because inside she knew that she was just as important as anyone else.

After college Margaret became a teacher. In her time she was known as one of the best elementary teachers in the county. And no one called her "teeny tiny Maggie" any more, though she still wasn't very big.

Those were the days when Margaret's life was filled with many things to do. There was not only her teaching but her husband and her family to think about. Margaret married a strapping six footer named Sam Trotter and together they raised four boys, all who grew to be over six feet tall. No one dared to call her tiny after that, especially when her boys were around.

And then of course there was her church and community work. Margaret directed the church choir and she led one of the county 4-H clubs. Margaret was very busy and happy for many years. And she never neglected to give thanks and praise to God.

But gradually over the years things began to change in Margaret's life. One by one her four tall sons grew up and went off to work in the city. She and Sam retired and spent their days working in the garden and their nights reading in front of the fireplace. How they enjoyed their retirement.

When Sam died, Margaret sold the big house where they had raised their boys and took a small apartment a few blocks from the church. She busied herself with volunteer work at the church and the hospital. And then it happened, just a week after her eighty-eighth birthday, Margaret fell and broke her hip. The doctor said that it would heal eventually but she wouldn't be able to take care of herself for a long time. She would have to go to a nursing home. Margaret didn't like the idea but she knew it was the best thing to do.

So there she was an eighty-eight-year-old woman trying to learn to walk again. It wouldn't have been so bad if they would have treated her with a little more respect. The staff was kind, courteous and professional in every way, but they talked down to her.

"Good morning, dearie," the nurse would say when she came in to get her up for breakfast. "And how are we feeling today?"

"How's my little Maggie doing?" the doctor said whenever he came by to check her hip.

And the new minister wasn't any better. Oh, he was a nice enough fellow, even though he did have a beard, but what right did he have to call her by her first name? The old minister always called her Mrs. Trotter.

Margaret felt so small she didn't know what to do. She became more and more depressed as each day passed. No one treated her like an adult, that is, no one except Herb the janitor. Herb was different from the others. He didn't seem to notice that she was old. At least it didn't make any difference in the way he treated her.

One day when Herb was mopping her room Margaret told him how small she was feeling. Herb said he understood. And he told Margaret, "What you need to do is get back to work."

"Why, I can't work," said Margaret, "I'm too old. Besides I can't even walk. Who would hire me?"

"Oh, I don't mean that kind of work," Herb said, "I mean God's work. God has work for us to do no matter how old or handicapped we may be. Get busy Margaret! There's no time to waste." And with that Herb wrung out his mop and headed out the door. Margaret didn't even have time to ask him what he meant.

All day long Margaret thought about what Herb had said. Maybe he was right. But what kind of work did God have for her to do?

Not long after that the social worker stopped by. She told Margaret that she had a favor to ask of her. She said, "There is a ninety-seven-year-old woman in 14B who has been feeling depressed lately. She is blind and confined to her bed. She has no family or friends who live near enough to visit regularly. I wondered if you would consider calling on her when you feel up to it?"

"Why, I would be delighted to call on her," Margaret said. Her prayers had been answered. This was the work God had for her to do. Margaret knew it immediately and she wondered why she hadn't thought of it herself.

She visited every day with the woman in 14B. Eleanor had been a teacher, too. Margaret read aloud to her from books they both enjoyed and it wasn't long until they became fast friends.

There were others that Margaret befriended, too. She made regular rounds every day even after she was well enough to go home to her apartment. Soon there were smiles and laughter around that nursing home like no one had ever seen before. No one felt small any more, least of all Margaret. She had never felt bigger and more important in her whole life.

And, oh yes, even the doctors and the nurses noticed the difference. They began to treat everyone with more respect.

The minister never did catch on, but then you know how ministers are.

The Devil in Willow Bluff

The Spirit immediately drove him into the wilderness. And he was in the wilderness forty days, tempted by Satan.

Mark 1:12-13b

And when the devil had ended every temptation, he departed from him until an opportune time.

Luke 4:13

Years ago there used to be a little church in a little town called Willow Bluff, and every Sunday the devil came alive there in the stories of the preacher and the Sunday School teachers. Whatever the text of the sermon and whatever the topic of the Sunday School lesson, the last word was always about Satan. He is everywhere, they said. Beware of his temptations, they warned. He will use any means available to snatch an unwary soul.

Whenever people gathered to socialize in that community there was always some talk about the devil. If someone was caught doing something he shouldn't have been doing, he would say, "The devil made me do it." If someone was mean and continually getting into trouble they would say, "He is full of the devil." If anything unexplainable happened someone was bound to say, "It's the devil's work." Some claimed that they had actually seen the devil.

There was one old Sunday School teacher who was particularly good at spinning these tales of devil woe. Her name was Agnes Woodley. She had been teaching the young people's class for over forty years. They loved to listen to her stories. She told about the serpent who tricked Adam and Eve in the Garden of Eden, and of the devil tempting Jesus in the wilderness, but the one the young people liked to hear her tell the most was about the day the devil came to church.

"One Sunday morning," Mrs. Woodley always began, "not too many years before all of you were born, the devil appeared in person right here on the main street of Willow Bluff. He walked straight into the church, strolled smoothly up the aisle as if going to church was something he did every Sunday, stepped up onto the platform and sat down in the place of honor, that empty chair next to the preacher where the guest evangelists always sit. He was very well dressed. He had on a blue suit, a white shirt, a bright red tie and shiny black shoes. He was a very fine figure of . . . a devil. It wasn't clear how everyone knew who he was, but we knew," she said. "There was no doubt about it, it was Old Scratch himself."

"Except for the devil's grand entrance," Mrs. Woodley said, "the service went along pretty much as usual. The devil joined in the singing, seemed to know all of the hymns by heart, and he even bowed his head during the prayers. When it came time for the sermon the devil got up to speak. The preacher started to object, but the devil said, 'Give me just two minutes and I'll be on my way.' The preacher looked at the congregation, and seeing no sign of protest, he nodded for the devil to go ahead.

"The devil stepped up to the pulpit, looked out warmly over all the worshipers, smiled sweetly, and then in a sonorous tone that suggested years of oratorical experience, he said, 'My dear friends, it's so good to be here with you today. I see so many familiar faces. I would like to take this opportunity to offer you a proposition which I think you will agree is in the best interest of your church and community. I will guarantee that all of your young people will be safe from drugs, alcohol, drunk driving, tragic accidents, suicide, premarital pregnancy, abortion, fornication, adultery and divorce, all of the things you worry about and preach against, if you will allow me one small consideration.'

"Here the devil paused, and waited until he could see that their interest was piqued. And then with the timing of a master salesman, he held them in that moment of expectation just long enough before he added, 'All I ask is that you allow me to cook the pancakes at your annual pancake supper, not every year, but once, let us say, every ten years or so.'

Now Willow Bluff Community Church was known for two things, preaching against the devil and their annual pancake suppers. People came from miles around to eat their pancakes. Some said their sourdough cakes were the best in the world. There is nothing like a stack of hot sourdough cakes smothered with fresh Willow Bluff sorghum. It was ambrosia. All of the young people knew this. The annual pancake supper was their favorite church activity. They got to help wait on tables, and more important, they got to eat. But that wasn't the reason that this was their favorite part of the story.

Mrs. Woodley always paused here to let the class feel the full effect of the devil's proposition. She wanted them to feel it the way their parents and grandparents felt it when they heard it from the devil's own lips. It didn't seem like too much to ask for that kind of guarantee. Some of them knew that it was just what their parents were looking for. How many times had they heard them say they would give anything to keep their kids safe from the evils of this corrupt modern world? What harm could it do if the devil cooked the pancakes every ten years or so? It was tempting, very tempting.

Then Mrs. Woodley went on, "No one knew what to do. It seemed like too good a deal to turn down. But how could they enter into an agreement with the devil?"

"While they were pondering all of this, Billy Chink got up and approached the devil. Billy was known as something of a trouble maker in the community, but his mother saw to it that he got to church every Sunday, and," Mrs. Woodley said, "he came regularly to my young people's class. Billy marched right up to the devil, looked him in the eye and said, 'We don't need to make any deals with you. Our Lord Jesus Christ died on the cross for us, and that is the only guarantee we need.'

"At this," she said, "the devil turned pale and began to slink out of the pulpit. Billy took out a water pistol and squeezed off a shot at point blank range. The devil ducked, dove down off the platform, scooted down the aisle, ran out the door and took off down the road as fast as he could go. But when he turned the corner he stopped, and he climbed up onto the bluff which overlooks the town, and to this day," Mrs. Woodley always said, "he sits there waiting and watching for an opportune time."

Molly's Glory

. . . if any man would come after me, let him deny himself and take up his cross and follow me. For whoever would save his life will lose it; and whoever loses his life for my sake and the gospel's will save it. For what does it profit a man, to gain the whole world and forfeit his life? For what can a man give in return for his life? For whoever is ashamed of me and my words in this adulterous and sinful generation, of him will the Son of man also be ashamed, when he comes in the glory of his Father with the holy angels.

Mark 8:34b-38

Molly McGinnis walked out the side door of the school building one day after school and saw something absolutely shocking. Her big brother, Sean, was sitting on top of a little boy about half his size and was beating his face with his fists. Blood was pouring out of the little boy's nose, but still Sean continued to hit and hit and hit.

At first Molly was stunned. She didn't know what to do or say. She stood in the doorway for what seemed like an eternity. It was only a moment, but a thousand thoughts raced through her mind. She had never seen Sean do anything like this before, and she couldn't imagine what the little boy could have done to make him so angry.

It came to her through a haze that she must do something to stop Sean. But what? There was no time to find a teacher and besides, how could she tell on her own brother?

And then she knew. It came to her in a flash. In the same instant she found herself running toward her brother. Without saying a word she threw herself on the ground beside the little boy. She rolled and slid her body in as close as she could get to the two boys, and then heaving with all of her little girl might, she put her face between the little boy's face and her brother's fists.

The next blow caught her right in the eye. Oh, how it hurt. Molly hurt like she had never hurt before. And then Sean stopped. He saw her and he saw what he had done.

They both helped the little boy get to his feet. Sean said he was sorry and gave the little boy his handkerchief to wipe off the blood.

Molly had a black eye for about six weeks. It was the blackest and bluest shiner anyone had ever seen. The kids at school all laughed and made fun of it. They thought Molly had been very foolish. But Sean and the little boy knew better. They had seen Molly in her glory.

A Wise Judge

Now Deborah, a prophetess, the wife of Lappidoth was judging Israel at that time. She used to sit under the palm of Deborah between Ramah and Bethel in the hill country of Ephraim; and the people of Israel came up to her for judgment.

Judges 4:4-5

Once upon a time there was a wise girl named Honey Bee, Honey Bee Rabinowitz. Isn't that a strange name? They called her Honey for short.

Honey was in the fifth grade at Bethel elementary school. She wasn't the prettiest girl in school; she was kind of skinny and she had a long nose with three freckles on the end of it, one in the middle and one on each side; and she was not the smartest girl in school. Susan Hilton was much smarter. She always got A's in math and English. Honey usually got B's and C's. But though she wasn't the prettiest girl in school or the smartest, Honey was the wisest girl. She was wiser than all of the girls and all of the boys, and probably wiser than most of the teachers.

Whenever someone had a problem, they would come to Honey and she would tell them what to do. She used to sit under the swing set on the playground during recess and if someone had a problem they would come and talk to her.

One day her cousin Freddie who was in the fifth grade came to see her. They called him Fast Freddie because he was the fastest runner in school.

Freddie told her that some of the big boys in the seventh and eighth grade class had been beating up on some of the little kids and stealing their lunch tickets. Just the day before they had pushed his little brother George down on the ground, taken his tickets and ripped his jacket. Freddie didn't know what to do.

Honey said, "I'll have to think about this." She didn't always give an immediate answer. Sometimes she went home and prayed about the problem.

That night she asked God what to do about the big boys who were bullying the little kids. The next morning, when she woke up, she knew just what to do.

She went to school and she told Fast Freddie to take five of his friends and go stand up to the bullies.

Freddie said, "I'll go if you go with me, but I won't go alone." Honey said, "Okay, I'll go with you if you are such a sissy and just see who puts a stop to this."

Freddie went and found his friends. They met Honey by the water fountain and then they went outside to take on the bullies. They found them behind the school. They were playing underneath the principal's window. The window was open.

About that time two little second grade boys came along. The big seventh and eighth grade boys grabbed them and were about to take their lunch tickets when Fast Freddie and his boys ran up to try to stop them. But before they could do anything the principal looked out the window and saw what was happening. She told them all to come to her office.

She sent the big boys home and called all their parents and told them what their sons had been doing. They never bothered anyone again.

Fast Freddie was the hero of the school for a while but one day after all of the excitement had passed, Honey reminded him that the bullies had been stopped because of the open window. "Who do you suppose opened the window?" she asked him. "Did you open it?" asked Freddie. "No, I didn't open the window," Honey told him, "but I know who did."

(Who do you think opened the window?)

Author's Note: *Judges 4:4-9 is an alternate text for the fourth Sunday of Lent added by The Inclusive Language Lectionary Committee in "An Inclusive Language Lectionary: Readings For Year B." According to the committee, ". . . it is appropriate to add certain lections about women that have not been included in the listing recommended by the North American Committee on Calendar and Lectionary." (The Cooperative Publication Association, 1987), p. 255.*

Dudley, The Dreary Donkey

And when they drew near to Jerusalem, to Beth-phage and Bethany, at the Mount of Olives, he sent two of his disciples, and said to them, "Go into the village opposite you, and immediately as you enter it you will find a colt tied, on which no one has ever sat; untie it and bring it.

Mark 11:1-2

Once upon a time there was a donkey named Dudley. He was known far and wide as Dudley, the dreary donkey, because he always looked sad. Wherever Dudley went his head hung down and his ears drooped so low they almost dragged on the ground. Droopy ears are a sure sign of unhappiness in donkeys.

Dudley had not always been dreary. When he was little he was as happy as any donkey could be. But then, one day, Dudley had a dream. It was a special dream. Dudley knew it was special, because it was unlike any other dream he had ever had before. And, what's more, Dudley knew, he just knew, that his special dream was going to come true.

In the dream Dudley saw himself carrying a very important man on his back. He was the most important man in the world. And as Dudley carried him along people cheered and cheered, and threw their coats down on the path in front of him.

When Dudley woke up, he was so sure that his special dream was going to come true that he went around and told all of his friends about it. Dudley was so excited that he thought his friends would be excited, too, but they didn't seem to understand. They laughed at him and made fun of him.

After that, wherever he went the other donkeys would point at him and say, "There goes Dudley the dreamer." And that's when Dudley became dreary. But he didn't give up hope. Deep down inside, Dudley knew that someday his dream would come true. Whenever someone came to the donkey pen Dudley's ears would prick up, and he would hold his breath, thinking this might be the day when his special dream would come true.

One day two men came to the donkey pen. They told the owner they wanted a donkey for a very special occasion. Immediately Dudley's ears pricked up, and he held his shoulders up high so that they would look wide and strong.

The two men looked over all of the donkeys carefully. They patted and poked and nodded and shook their heads until finally they came to Dudley. "This is the one," one of the men said to the other one. "Yes, no doubt about it," said the other man, "I think the master will be very pleased with this donkey."

Dudley could hardly contain his joy. He wanted to jump and kick and hee-haw all over the pen. But, instead he just smiled to himself and walked along as if it were any ordinary day.

When they got to the edge of the city, a very wise and gentle looking man, dressed in a white robe, came over and got up on Dudley's back. He patted Dudley on the head and spoke softly in his ear. "He sure doesn't act as if he were the most important man in the world," Dudley thought to himself, "Maybe this isn't the day my dream will come true after all."

But, when they came into the city all the doubts left Dudley's mind. There were thousands of people lining the streets. They waved palm branches and shouted hosanna. Some of the people threw their coats on the ground for Dudley to walk on.

Dudley held his head up high and his ears stuck straight up toward the sky. He knew that his special dream had come true. He couldn't wait to get back to the pen and tell his friends that he had carried the most important man in the world. Now they would know that he wasn't just a dreamer, and nobody would ever again call him Dudley, the dreary donkey.

The Comforting Word

But when Christ appeared as a high priest of the good things that have come, then through the greater and more perfect tent (not made with hands, that is, not of this creation) he entered once for all into the Holy Place, taking not the blood of goats and calves but his own blood, thus securing an eternal redemption. For if the sprinkling of defiled persons with the blood of goats and bulls and with the ashes of a heifer sanctifies for the purification of the flesh, how much more shall the blood of Christ, who through the eternal Spirit offered himself without blemish to God, purify your conscience from dead works to serve the living God.

Hebrews 9:11-14

Howard Jackman had a way with words. Everyone said so. He was not a speech maker. He didn't sound like a politician or a preacher. But he had a way of putting thoughts into words that touched people deeply. Howard probably could have gone anywhere and done anything he wanted to do. He graduated at the head of his high school class and received an honor scholarship which would have paid most of his way through college. But Howard didn't want to go to college. He wanted to be a cheesemaker, like his father. And that is what he did. He married a local girl, they had a couple of kids, he made prize-winning cheese, and enjoyed the simple life in Willow Bluff. On Saturdays he went fishing or hunting: squirrels, ducks, geese, pheasants, whatever happened to be in season. On Sundays he and his family were always in church. Sometimes, when the preacher was absent they would call on him to give the sermon.

When Howard's best friend, John Whitcomb, committed suicide, John's wife, Ellen, asked him if he would say a few words at the funeral. Howard said he would.

The day came, and Howard didn't have the slightest idea what he was going to say. He sat silently through the opening part of the service, not looking at the casket or at John's three little sons hanging onto their mother in the front row pew, until it came time for him to speak. Then he took it all in as he walked slowly up to the front. He paused for a moment to put his hand on the casket before he stepped up onto the platform and stood facing the congregation behind the casket, about two feet from the pulpit.

"I'm not sure I can say anything at all," he said. "It hurts so much I can hardly stand to be here. I feel like running away, but there's nowhere to run. I keep trying to push time back in my mind, thinking there must be some mistake, that I will wake up and everything will be all right.

"John Whitcomb was the kindest, sweetest, gentlest man I have ever known. I love him like a brother. I don't want to let him go.

"Johnny and I went squirrel hunting after dinner on Saturday. We walked the ridges up on the Gray place. Every once in a while we would stop and sit in the sun under an oak tree, and talk about fishing. It's funny, when we were fishing we always talked about hunting, and when we were hunting we always talked about fishing. Sometimes when the fish weren't biting or game was scarce we would sit down on a log and Johnny would recite a psalm and then we would chew on it for a while. Johnny loved to repeat the psalms. I don't think many people knew that. He knew a good many of them by heart.

"We saw only one squirrel all afternoon. Johnny saw him first, but he didn't shoot. He didn't even raise his gun. It was a black squirrel. We had seen only one of its kind around here once before and that was way over on Little Willow. Johnny pointed his finger and we watched as the squirrel scampered beneath the tree. When his mouth was full of acorns he sprang onto one of the biggest oaks, ran up the trunk, jumped from limb to limb and finally deposited his load in a tangle of leaves at the top of the tree.

"It's going to be a long winter," Johnny said.

"We had turned to go when suddenly we were aware of something large and dark over our heads, and we heard a whoosh of wings ascending on the air. We looked up and there was a great hawk winging off into the blue with the black squirrel gripped securely in his talons. We stood in awe for several moments and then Johnny said something which at the time struck me as rather peculiar. He said, 'The children of men take refuge in the shadow of thy wings.'

"I knew it was probably from one of the Psalms but I didn't know what he meant by it. He was quiet after that and I could tell he didn't want to talk for a while so I didn't question him about it. We walked in silence the rest of the afternoon, soaking up the sights, sounds and smells of the woods. When we reached the line fence on the north end of the ridge, Johnny turned to me and said, 'Let's go home. Ellen will have supper on in a little bit.'

"It was dark by the time we got back to the house. We ate supper and sat at the table drinking coffee and talking for a long time. About 9:30 we heard an awful racket out by the barn. Johnny went out to see what it was. In about two minutes he was back. 'Grab the broom,' he said. 'There's a stray cat caught in a rat trap out by the corn crib.' When we got to the cat he pulled away, tearing some of the flesh on his leg. 'Push down on him,' Johnny said. 'Hold him still so I can let him loose.' I put the broom on the cat and held him tight against the ground. Johnny squeezed the trap's release mechanism and the jaws popped open. The cat got to his feet, licked his wounded leg, and took off as fast as he could go.

"As we walked back to the house Johnny said, 'Sometimes I feel like that cat in the trap. It's like something's got ahold of me, and there is nothing I can do to get free of it. The doctor calls it depression. He says the medication will help in time, but I don't know. I just don't know.'

Howard paused, raised his eyes, and then in a softer, quieter voice said, "I don't know either. I don't know if I ever will. I will always wonder if there was something I could have done.

"After Ellen called, I got out the Bible and looked up that verse in the Psalms. I had to hunt and hunt. I finally found it in the middle of the thirty-sixth Psalm. It goes something like this." He began to recite the words slowly, almost ponderously, laboring over each word as if retrieving it from some remote place deep in his soul.

> . . . *man and beast thou savest, O Lord. How precious is thy steadfast love . . . The children of men take refuge in the shadow of thy wings. They feast on the abundance of thy house, and thou givest them drink from the river of thy delights. For with thee is the fountain of life; in thy light do we see light. O continue thy steadfast love to those who know thee, and thy salvation to the upright of heart!*

It was quiet in the church long after Howard sat down. Several moments passed before anyone moved or looked away. And when at last the preacher's voice called them back for the singing of the closing hymn, there was in their eyes a renewed sense of hope, and in their hearts the comforting word.

A Church in Need of Aid

Surely he has borne our griefs and carried our sorrows; yet we esteemed him stricken, smitten by God and afflicted. But he was wounded for our transgressions, he was bruised for our iniquities; upon him was the chastisement that made us whole, and with his stripes we were healed.

Isaiah 53:4-5

Which of these three do you think, proved neighbor to the man who fell among robbers?

Luke 10:36

Charlie Stevenson moved to town the day after they decided to close the church, although he didn't hear about it until he went to worship the following Sunday. The church was almost full on that particular day. It was the beginning of a kind of extended wake which was to last three months. That was when Pastor Timmerman was scheduled to retire for the second and last time and the church doors were to be closed for good. He had come to be their pastor after his first retirement from a big city church. The part-time arrangement, the low salary and the provision of a parsonage met both his and the church's needs. Now with his imminent departure, the ministry of the dwindling congregation seemed to be at an end. They had decided to close the church doors rather than to go on with what had become a constant struggle to pay the bills and, perhaps more important, to be free of the guilt of not being able to pay their fair share of the denomination's mission budget, a responsibility they had not been able to fulfill for a number of years.

Everybody came that first Sunday after the decision to pay their last respects to the old white frame building and to a way of life that had existed in their little community for over a hundred years. It seemed that the church had always been there. It was the only church in the village. Its presence had been important even to those who never came to worship. It was a center of community life not only on those occasions when weddings and funerals were celebrated there, but also during election day dinners, 4-H Club meetings and numerous other community functions. So everybody came that first Sunday after the vote to mourn the death of their church.

To an outsider that day it would have appeared that the church was full of life. Charlie Stevenson didn't know quite what to make of it. He had come with the full intention of transferring his membership as soon as the congregation and the pastor were willing to receive him. The church was within walking distance of the house he had rented and it was of his denomination. It never occurred to him that he would join anywhere else. Now what was he going to do? Did it make sense to join a dying church?

Charlie decided that he would wait and see. In the meantime he could see no reason for not becoming involved in the things he had always done in church. He asked about Bible study and choir practice, and yes, he would be interested in playing on the church softball team. He liked to play second base, but would be glad to fill in wherever there was a need.

People took to Charlie immediately. People always had. He was a tall man, well over six feet, with broad shoulders, a full head of light brown hair and a smile that never quit. Charlie seemed to like everyone. People couldn't help liking him because they knew he liked them.

When word got out that Charlie was coming to choir practice the soprano section almost doubled. Two eligible young women with modest vocal talents who hadn't been to practice in several months suddenly found themselves free of all pressing social engagements. They said they had come for the choir's last hurrah, but they had a hard time keeping their eyes on the music and not on Charlie. The second week Charlie brought the centerfielder and the shortstop from the softball team.

73

Everybody knew they were wonderful singers, but it was Charlie who had said to them, "Why don't you come sing with us? It's great fun." So they had come.

It was the same at the Thursday night Bible Study. Six or seven was the usual average attendance. Sometimes they would have a dozen or more at the beginning of a series, or when they met at Mabel Robinson's house. Mabel was the best dessert maker in town and she had the biggest and the fanciest house. People liked to go there just to see her antique furniture and to ogle the crystal chandelier which her grandfather had had shipped over from Paris. Mabel was usually ready for anything, but even she wasn't prepared for the twenty-three people who showed up for Bible Study that second week after Charlie moved to town. There were the seven regulars, the pastor and his wife who came only once in a while, five of the irregulars who had started out with the class at the beginning of the series but had slipped away after a week or two, the two newly-enthused sopranos, the centerfielder and the shortstop, two of Mabel's good friends who had come to help serve dessert, Charlie, and a couple of guys who worked with him in the office down at the mill. Mabel had to scramble to find enough chairs for everyone. And she had to sneak out to the store during the opening prayer to get some extra sherbet to go with her lemon chiffon cake.

The amazing thing was that this sudden rise in attendance at choir practice, at Bible Study and at worship was no passing phenomenon. It grew steadily every week. People were getting involved who hadn't been in church for anything but a special community event in years. A couple of families who had been attending a bigger church over in the county seat came "back home" to worship, "for old time's sake" they said. But everyone could tell they had been caught up in the new spirit, too. It was almost enough to make everyone forget that the church was about to be closed.

Then Charlie got sick. Word got out that he had a fast-spreading cancer. People could hardly believe it. Charlie who was so full of life, the man who had almost single-handedly brought the church back to life — dying? It couldn't be true. Mabel and one of the other older women decided to go over and see how he was after the pastor announced his illness in church that Sunday. It was next to the last Sunday in May, just five weeks before the church was scheduled to be closed.

They found Charlie in bed, too weak to respond to their knock on the door. Mabel went right in and when she saw the state he was in she sent her friend to call the doctor. The doctor wanted him to go to the hospital, but Charlie said he had been through all of that before and this time he was going to stay at home. "Well then," Mabel said, "you will need a nurse. I'll go and get my things."

"Wait just a minute," Charlie said, "you don't know what you're getting into. You need to know that I have AIDS and that I'm gay."

Mabel didn't know what to say. She was clearly taken aback. She had never in her wildest imaginings thought that she would have to face anything like this. Finally, after a long pause, she turned to the doctor and said, "Doc, what do I have to do to protect myself?" When the doctor had told her, she went straight home, got her overnight bag, brought her favorite pillow, made a bed on the couch and then set about caring for Charlie's needs. She offered to call his family, but Charlie said it would be better if she didn't. He gave her the number though, "Just in case," he said.

Mabel stayed by Charlie's bedside night and day for the next eight days. She made sure that no one stayed too long when they came for a visit. She even chased the pastor out once when she could see that Charlie was getting tired.

Charlie died on Memorial Day just before sunrise. When Mabel called his family they said they didn't want anything to do with him. They said, "Charlie made his bed, now let him lie in it." They told her she could make any arrangements she wanted, said Charlie had plenty of money to pay for everything. They didn't even want his things, said to give everything away.

When the word got out that Charlie's family didn't want him and weren't coming to the funeral the church took it as a challenge. It didn't matter that Charlie was gay or that he had died of AIDS, he was their Charlie and by God they were going to see that he was buried properly.

Everybody came to the funeral. Pastor Timmerman gave the finest sermon anyone had ever heard him preach. The choir sang like they had never sung before and when the boys from the softball team carried the casket out of the church the centerfielder led the congregation in singing "Blest Be The Tie That Binds." Tears flowed freely that day. No one who was present had any doubt that "the fellowship of kindred minds is like to that above."

The next day after the funeral the bishop got a call from Sam Eberly, the church's lay leader. "We've changed our minds," Sam said. "We want to keep the church open."

Diane's Story

*But Mary stood weeping outside the tomb, and as
she wept she stooped to look into the tomb; and she
saw two angels in white, sitting where the body of
Jesus had lain, one at the head and one at the feet.
They said to her, "Woman, why are you weeping?"
She said to them, "Because they have taken away
my Lord, and I do not know where they have laid
him." Saying this, she turned around and saw Jesus
standing, but she did not know that it was Jesus.
Jesus said to her, "Woman, why are you weeping?
Whom do you seek?" Supposing him to be the
gardener, she said to him, "Sir if you have carried
him away, tell me where you have laid him, and I
will take him away." Jesus said to her, "Do not hold
me, for I have not yet ascended to my Father and
your Father; to my God and your God." Mary Mag-
dalene went and said to the disciples, "I have seen
the Lord"; and she told them that he had said these
things to her.*

John 20:11-18

Diane was eight years old when her brother Larry died.
Larry was nine. They had always been close. Diane followed
her older brother everywhere. They helped their Dad and Mom
on the farm, cared for the animals, chased each other around
the buildings, played hide and seek in the haymow and ram-
bled through the meadow and the woods behind the barn.
Diane would confess years later that she had been a bit of a
tomboy.

One day Diane was invited to go with two of her girl friends
to a baseball game. Larry asked to go along but Diane said it

was just for girls and they didn't want any boys tagging along. In the end their parents decided that this time Larry would stay at home.

When they arrived at the game, there was a message that they should return home at once. Larry had been killed in a tractor accident. He was riding on the back of a tractor driven by one of the neighbor's hired men. The tractor had hit a bump, throwing Larry forward and down under one of the big rear wheels. His father who was following behind on another tractor, picked him up and rushed him to a hospital where he died a short time later.

Diane's first thought was, "I'm all alone. I'll have to do everything by myself now." And then she felt a terrible, agonizing, painful guilt in the pit of her stomach.

"If I had let Larry go to the game this wouldn't have happened."

On the third night after the funeral, Diane wakened suddenly, sat up in her bed and saw Larry sitting on the window sill across the room. Several moments passed as they sat there just looking at each other. "And then," Diane said, "Larry vanished right before my eyes."

When she told her family later, Diane said, "No one doubted me."

Diane says that she still gets goose bumps when she tells this story. And she says, "To this day when I close my eyes I can see Larry sitting there just as he was that night when he appeared in my room."

If you were to ask Diane why she thinks Larry came to her, she would tell you, "I felt it was his way of saying goodbye and God's way of showing me he is alive."

Author's Note: *(Diane Henderson related this story to the author in May of 1988. It appears here with her permission.)*

Moving

Jesus said to her, "Do not hold me, for I have not yet ascended to the Father; but go to my brethren and say to them, I am ascending to my Father and your Father, to my God and your God."

John 20:17

Once upon a time there was a little girl named Marcie who lived in a big old house with her Mom and Dad and her Grandma Elizabeth. Marcie's house was next to a deep river on the far side of town. It had big rooms with lots of low windows, so low that Marcie could see out wherever she went without standing on her tiptoes. And it had lots of nooks and corners where a little girl could hide and pretend to be whoever or whatever she wanted to be. Some of the rooms had connecting closets so you could go into a closet in one room and come out in another. Marcie loved to run through the closets and up and down the stairs all through the house. Sometimes she ran all the way up to the attic and when she felt really brave she would go down into the dark basement and pretend she was exploring a cave.

There were many interesting places in Marcie's big old house. But her favorite place was Grandma Elizabeth's room. It had a fireplace and a big brass bed. At the foot of the bed there was an old black trunk filled with Grandma's keepsakes. In the corner across from the bed there was a bay window with hanging plants and oodles of purple violets. On the walls there were pictures of Grandma's children and grandchildren. There were so many pictures that you could hardly see the wallpaper. Grandma loved to show Marcie her pictures and tell about each one.

Best of all there was Grandma Elizabeth. She was getting old and she could hardly walk. So most of the time she sat in her rocking chair by the fireplace and knitted mittens and scarves for Marcie and all of her other grandchildren. That was the nice thing about Grandma Elizabeth, Marcie always knew where to find her.

Whenever Marcie needed to talk to someone she would go to Grandma Elizabeth's room and climb up on her lap. She was always glad to see her and she always listened very closely to everything Marcie had to say. Sometimes she would tell her a story. Marcie loved Grandma Elizabeth's stories. She thought her Grandma told the best stories in the world.

One day, Marcie's Daddy came home and announced that they were moving. He said, they were going to a new house across the river near the factory where he worked. They would be closer to the downtown and just a few blocks from Marcie's school.

At first Marcie couldn't believe her ears. It couldn't be true. How could she leave her big old house? And where would Grandma Elizabeth go? Would there be room for her in the new house? A thousand questions ran through Marcie's mind. It just wasn't fair. Why couldn't things stay the way they were? Marcie ran up to her room, slammed the door, threw herself on the bed and cried and cried.

When she stopped crying Marcie decided to go see Grandma Elizabeth. Grandma Elizabeth was glad to see her, as usual. Marcie climbed up into her warm lap and snuggled up close.

After awhile she said, "I don't want to move. I want to live in this house some more."

Grandma Elizabeth gave Marcie a big hug and then she told her an old, old, story. She said, "Marcie, do you remember the caterpillar we saw last spring?" "Yes," said Marcie, "I remember. It was green with white and black stripes and it crawled on tiny little legs." "That's right," said Grandma. "And do you remember that after a while the caterpillar became a chrysalis and hung from a milkweed pod for a long time. And then one day the chrysalis opened and out came

80

a bright orange and black monarch butterfly. The caterpillar with tiny legs turned into a beautiful creature with wings which took it way up in the sky. Do you suppose" said Grandma, "that that little caterpillar might have felt the way you feel when it had to move from legs to wings? He liked being a caterpillar and he didn't understand why he couldn't always be a caterpillar, but after he got his wings he thought how glorious it is to be a butterfly."

A few years later when Marcie was a big girl of ten, long after they had moved to their new house and Marcie had come to love it, even more than the old house, they got a call from the nursing home where Grandma Elizabeth lived. The nurse on the phone said to come quickly, that Grandma Elizabeth was very sick.

When they got to her room Grandma Elizabeth looked pale and weak, but she smiled when she saw them. They all hugged her and told her that they loved her. Then Grandma Elizabeth took hold of Marcie's hand and said, "Marcie, do you remember the butterfly?" "Yes," said Marcie, "I remember." Grandma Elizabeth smiled again and then she said something that Marcie would remember as long as she lived. She said, "In the spring when you see butterflies dancing in the sunlight, think of me and smile."

Grandma Elizabeth died later that afternoon. Marcie and her family were very sad for a long time. Sometimes Marcie cried. But in the spring when she saw butterflies dancing in the sunlight, she would think of Grandma Elizabeth and smile.

Heaven Bound

Beloved, we are God's children now; it does not yet appear what we shall be, but we know that when he appears we shall be like him, for we shall see him as he is. And every one who thus hopes in him purifies himself as he is pure.

1 John 3:2-3

Truly I say to you, whatever you bind on earth shall be bound in heaven, and whatever you loose on earth shall be loosed in heaven.

Matthew 18:18

There was once a successful businessman who was the bitter enemy of another successful businessman in the same town. They both sold shoes and their stores stood side by side on the main street. They went to the same church. They belonged to some of the same clubs, but they never spoke. They stayed away from each other as much as possible. This was somewhat ironic because they had been boyhood chums. Everybody said they were inseparable, more like brothers than good friends.

Their enmity began over a conflict of interest. They both fell in love with the same girl. Even so everything would have been fine except she dated one first, became engaged to him, then jilted him to marry the other.

There was an ugly scene one day when they came together in front of one of the local watering holes. They shouted and raved, called each other loathsome names and nearly came to blows.

Each one swore that he would never speak to the other again. And they didn't. Even when their wives died, as it happened, just a few months apart, they went to the services, each nodded to the other in a polite, public way, but they did not speak.

Now one of them was dying and just before he died he had a vision. He saw an angel come to greet him and welcome him to heaven. He told the angel how delighted he was to be there. He had never been absolutely sure that heaven was the place where he was going to go. He had always been afraid that he might go to the other place. But here he was, and all was well. He asked the angel to show him around. The angel said he would be delighted. After all, that was his job.

He led the man down the main street of a small town. It was a very pleasant looking town with trees and benches, clean swept sidewalks and curbs, very much like the little town where he had lived all his life.

They came to a shoe store and the angel said, "This is where you are going to work."

They walked around inside and looked at the goods. The stock included all the latest styles, the very best shoes that could be had anywhere.

The businessman expressed his great pleasure. He said, "I always wondered what I would do in heaven. I am glad to see it will be what I do best."

When they walked outside he was surprised to discover that there was another shoe store right next door to his. "Whose store is that?" he asked the angel.

"Why, that will be your friend's store when he gets here in just a few years," the angel replied. "You will be working side by side just as you always have."

The businessman awoke with a start. Immediately he sent for his boyhood friend. When his friend arrived he embraced him and told him how sorry he was for all the wasted years. Then he said to his friend, "I want you to do me a favor. I want you to take over my store, and as neither of us have any children, when you come to the time when you can't take care of it any longer, I want you to sell it and give the money to our church."

Then he died in the arms of his friend, smiling, because he knew that their friendship would never end.

Drastic Measures

No man has ever seen God; if we love one another,
God abides in us and his love is perfected in us.

1 John 4:12

Jeremy Wagner was angry. Kathy had bumped into him while he was standing next to the water fountain and he immediately hauled off and slugged her on the ear. Kathy cried and cried, and when she stopped crying, she went down the hall to find the teacher.

Now Kathy was no tattletale. She could take her licks with the best of them. But this was just too much. Jeremy was always hitting someone or kicking someone and sometimes even worse. One day he bit George Larson right on the end of the nose so hard that George was sure he'd lost his nose forever. And if he wasn't physically assaulting someone, he was teasing them. Jeremy never had anything good to say about anyone. It seemed that he was always angry. Kathy decided something had to be done.

When she walked into Mr. Sanders' room he took one look at her face and said, "Jeremy again?"

She nodded her head. "You've got to do something about him, Mr. Sanders. It's not safe to walk the halls when he's around."

Mr. Sanders said, "Thank you, Kathy. I'll see what I can do." His voice sounded confident and reassuring, but inside Mr. Sanders wasn't so sure. He had talked to Jeremy almost every day since the beginning of the school year. He had sent him to the principal's office so many times he thought there must be a beaten path by now. The principal had done everything he could think of to make him change his ways. He made him stay after school. He talked to his parents. He even suspended him once for three days. Jeremy was the only kid in the whole history of the grade school who had ever been suspended. Nothing seemed to work. Jeremy just got meaner and meaner.

Finally Mr. Sanders decided the situation called for drastic measures. He called Jeremy into his room and told him to stand perfectly still in front of his desk.

"Now, Jeremy," he said, "I've told you before, you've got to stop hurting people. The principal has told you and your Mom and Dad have told you. We have punished you in every way the law allows and you still insist on hurting people. Jeremy Wagner, I want you to listen to me now and listen good. I am going to have to deal with you in a way that you have never been dealt with before. I want you to come to my room every day after school for the next two weeks. Be here at exactly three o'clock."

"But I'll miss the bus," said Jeremy.

"The bus doesn't leave until 3:15," said Mr. Sanders. "You be here at three o'clock. I'll make sure you catch the bus on time."

The next day at three o'clock Jeremy was there right on time, and he was scared. He didn't know what Mr. Sanders was going to do but he knew it was going to be something terrible.

When Mr. Sanders came in he walked right up to Jeremy and without saying a word, gave him a big . . . hug! And before Jeremy could say or do anything he said, "That will be all for today, Jeremy. See you tomorrow, same time."

The next day at three o'clock Mr. Sanders did exactly the same thing. On Wednesday Mr. Sanders did the same thing again, and after the hug he looked Jeremy right in the eye and said, "You know, Jeremy, even though you get into trouble all of the time, I think that underneath you are really a pretty good guy." Jeremy didn't say anything, but he knew something inside himself was beginning to change.

On Friday when Mr. Sanders hugged Jeremy, Jeremy hugged him back. He hadn't meant to; he just couldn't help himself. It seemed the natural thing to do.

The next week was the same thing all over again. Jeremy went to Mr. Sanders' room every day at three o'clock. Mr. Sanders gave him a big hug and every day now Jeremy hugged him back.

On Friday Jeremy was reluctant to go see Mr. Sanders. He knew it was the last day of his punishment and strange as it seemed, he didn't want it to end. Tears filled his eyes as Mr. Sanders hugged him for the last time. Jeremy decided he wouldn't let go. He clung to Mr. Sanders with all his might.

Mr. Sanders held Jeremy close for a long time. After a while Jeremy said, "No one ever hugs me at home. They just yell at me and tell me what a bad boy I am. But I know I'm not a bad boy. Not really."

"No, you're not a bad boy," said Mr. Sanders. "You just act like one sometimes. Maybe you can learn to act differently so that people will know what you're really like."

Jeremy stepped back from Mr. Sanders and wiped the last tears from his eyes. "I'll try to be good, Mr. Sanders. Honest I will."

"One more thing, Jeremy," said Mr. Sanders. "You don't have to come here every day at three o'clock anymore, but I'll be here anytime you need me."

Kathy and the other kids could hardly believe their eyes when they saw Jeremy walking down the hall that day. He wasn't hitting anyone; he wasn't kicking; he wasn't biting; he wasn't teasing. He was doing something they had never seen him do before. He was smiling. Jeremy Wagner wasn't angry anymore.

Greater Love

This is my commandment, that you love one another as I have loved you. Greater love has no man than this that a man lay down his life for his friends.
John 15:12

There was once a little girl who didn't have any friends. Her name was Hattie. But Hattie wasn't really a "little" girl. You see, she was the tallest girl in her class. She was three inches taller than the next tallest girl, and she was five inches taller than all of the boys. And what was worse, Hattie was new at school and everyone made fun of her. They called her "giraffe legs," and they laughed whenever she bumped her head on the swing set. Hattie didn't know what to do, so she would just run behind the school building and cry.

One day, Sean noticed one of the other kids making fun of Hattie, and he remembered that he had been treated the same way when he first moved to town. You see, Sean was short for his age, and the kids used to call him, "Sean, Sean, the leprechaun." Sean remembered how bad that had made him feel, and he decided right then and there that he was going to be Hattie's friend.

So, that afternoon, after school, Sean sneaked away from the other boys and walked with Hattie all the way to his house. Hattie was a little suspicious at first that it might be some kind of trick, but when Sean told her that he knew just how she felt, she thought it was all right. Then, when Sean invited her in to meet his sisters, Betty and Lois, she was delighted.

The next day at school things were entirely different. When the other kids saw Hattie playing with Sean and his sisters, they didn't tease her anymore. In fact, they wanted to play too, and pretty soon Hattie had more friends than she could count on her fingers. As for Sean, he went back to playing with the boys, but he was happy that he had helped someone who needed a friend.

Where the Story Never Ends

And this is the testimony, that God gave us eternal life, and this life is in his son.

1 John 5:11

In my Father's house are many rooms; if it were not so, I would have told you that I go to prepare a place for you, I will come again and will take you to my-self, that where I am you may be also.

John 14:2-3

An old man lay dying. His children and grandchildren were gathered all around. One by one he bid them farewell, leaving each one with his blessing and love. When he came at last to the youngest grandchild, he said, "Now, where is my little one?"

"Here I am," the little boy called as he jumped out of his mother's arms, climbed up onto the bed, and plopped himself down beside the old man. "I'm right here, Grandpa."

Neither of them said anything at first. The little boy took hold of one of the old man's tired hands, and, as he had often done in their play together, he tugged at the gold ring on his third finger. After a while, without lifting his eyes from the ring, he said, "Are you going to heaven, Grandpa?"

"Yes, little one," the old man replied, "I'm going to be with Grandma in that place that Jesus prepared for us."

There was a long silence as the little boy pondered what the old man had said. Then he raised himself up, and this time, looking deep into his grandfather's eyes, he asked, "Grandpa, where is heaven?"

The old man smiled and playfully ran his fingers through the little boy's curly brown hair. "Do you remember how you used to sit on my lap and beg me to tell you a story? You would say, 'Tell me a long, long one, Grandpa. I want it to go on and on forever.' "

The little boy's eyes were shining now, and he said, "Yes, I remember."

"Well," the old man sighed, "Heaven is like that. Heaven is where the story never ends."

The Town Pray-er

Likewise the spirit helps us in our weakness; for we do not know how to pray as we ought, but the Spirit himself intercedes for us with sighs too deep for words. And he who searches the hearts of men knows what is the mind of the Spirit, because the Spirit intercedes for the saints according to the will of God.

Romans 8:26-27

There was once a woman in our town who was known as the praying lady. Every community has persons who serve unofficially in certain positions, like the town fix-it man who can fix anything from sump pumps to screen doors, or the community singer who is called upon to solo at every wedding and funeral. The nature of these positions will vary according to the available talent. Esther Langford was our town pray-er. Nobody could pray like Esther. She had a way of putting into words what everyone was thinking and feeling. And not just ordinary words but beautiful poetic phrases so lovely that God could not help but be moved to attend to whatever person or concern was the subject of Esther's petition. So whenever there was going to be a special celebration, whether a wedding anniversary, a class reunion or the annual election day dinner, Esther was called upon to give the prayer.

This was a source of more than a little irritation to the various itinerant preachers who came to serve our little Protestant church. Preachers, as a rule, have a monopoly on the praying business. They are accustomed to having first refusal rights to the prayers at every public gathering. Some of them count on it. It's a way of getting free meals, one of the small perks of the preaching profession. Consequently, most

91

preachers can offer up a prayer at a moment's notice, although younger preachers are not usually as quick on their feet as older preachers. They tend to start slow and finish fast. If you are real hungry and if you have a choice, you would be best advised to choose a young preacher to say the grace. You can be sure that you will get to eat a lot sooner. Old preachers tend to go on and on. One certain way of telling the age of preachers is by the length of their prayers.

We had one old preacher who came to our church near the end of his ministry who gave the longest prayers anyone had ever heard. His pastoral prayers were almost as long as his sermons, and his sermons were way too long. This may have been because he didn't get to do much praying outside the Sunday service. Esther did most of that. I think those interminable pastoral prayers may have been his way of getting even.

It is written in scripture that God listens to the prayers of a righteous person. This certainly seemed to be true in Esther's case. She was a genuinely good person, thoughtful, kind, generous, willing to share whatever she had with anyone who was in need. Everybody knew that if God listened to anyone, God surely listened to Esther.

One summer during a long drought she was asked to pray for rain. That was the year of the great flood. The very next day after Esther prayed the heavens opened and precipitation came down in buckets. Ten inches of rain fell in three hours. We almost lost the town bridge. No one ever forgot it and no one ever asked Esther to pray for rain again.

There was a period of time when Esther didn't do any public praying. When people approached her she would say, "Thank you for asking, but I'm just not able to do it anymore." Years later, before she died, Esther told us that she went through a time of doubt. She said she didn't know what happened, but for a while she wasn't able to pray either publicly or privately. Esther said this was very unusual because, throughout her life, she had prayed daily first thing every morning and last thing every night.

What's more she said she wasn't sleeping well. Every night she had the same disturbing dream. At the end of the dream she would wake up, usually at about three o'clock in the morning and then try as she might, she wasn't able to go back to sleep.

Esther said this went on for weeks and weeks. She was absolutely miserable and afraid to tell anyone for fear of what they might think. Town pray-er indeed! What a laugh. She wondered if she ever really had known how to pray.

What was she going to do? The lack of sleep began to take a toll on her health. She decided that she had to do something. She thought of going to the preacher, but what would he think? Maybe he would think she had been a fraud all of these years. She tried sleeping pills, but they left her feeling "doped up" as she said, and more miserable than before. She had to talk to someone, but who? Who could she trust with the secret of her terrible misery?

Then it came to her. She would go to confession. She had only been inside the Catholic church for weddings and funerals, but she knew where the confessional booths were and she knew that Father Lempke heard confessions every Thursday night.

The next Thursday night Esther parked her car across the street from St. Killian's and waited until the last Catholic had left the building. She was shaking as she made her way to the confessional. She wasn't sure what she was going to say. Everything seemed strange: the high cathedral ceiling, the lighted candles in front of the statue of the Virgin, and the crucifix on the wall behind the altar; the smell of incense and warm wax was different from the musty smell of the little Protestant churches she was used to. All of it seemed to be saying, "You don't belong here. This is a holy place." But she forced herself to go on.

When she got into the confessional Esther knelt down and said, "Bless me Father, for I have sinned." That much she knew from the movies. But she didn't know what to say after that, so she finally blurted out, "I'm a Protestant. I don't really know how to do this. I didn't know where else to go, so I came here hoping you would help me with my problem. I hope that's all right."

Father Lempke must have thought, "The Protestants are beginning to see the light, they are starting to come to me for confession." But if he was surprised he didn't let on. He told Esther it was perfectly all right, he would be glad to listen. Then, Esther poured out her whole story, town pray-er and all.

The priest listened and when she had finished he said, "My dear woman, do you know the story of Samuel in the Old Testament?" Esther said that she did. There wasn't anyone in our community who knew the Bible better than Esther did.

The priest said, "Do you remember how God spoke to Samuel when he was a young boy?"

"Yes," Esther said, "I remember."

"Did it ever occur to you," the priest asked, "that God might be trying to tell you something? The next time you wake up in the middle of the night, do what Samuel did."

Esther hadn't known what to expect in a Catholic confessional, but she certainly hadn't expected this. As soon as she got home she looked up the story in 1 Samuel to refresh her memory as to what it was exactly that Samuel had done. It was just as she remembered.

That night she had the same dream she had been having for several weeks. In the dream everyone in town was chasing her through the woods and crying out, "Pray for us, pray for us!" To escape her pursuers she ran into a dark cave where she found herself being drawn along a winding tunnel. The tunnel came out in a large cavern as big as a cathedral and filled with a host of statue-like formations which glimmered and shimmered in the darkness. They were covered with sparkling crystals and appeared to be reaching out to her, bidding her to stop and take in all of their beauty. But the voices of the prayer-seekers were still ringing in her ears. She ran on down through another tunnel to a cavern that was bigger and more lovely than the one before. She wanted desperately to stop and allow herself to be filled with its beauty, but the voices persisted, growing louder and louder, their echoes resounding from wall to wall. "Pray for us, pray for us!" And so she ran on through cavern after cavern, each one grander and more glorious than the one before, until at last she was pulled by some mysterious and irresistible force over a ledge into a great abyss. She felt herself falling and falling and it was at this point that she always woke up.

And that night when she woke up, she did what Samuel did. She said, "Speak, for thy servant hears."

And then it came to her, a verse out of her memory, ". . . the Spirit helps us in our weakness; for we do not know how to pray as we ought, but the Spirit . . . intercedes for us with sighs too deep for words."

"What a relief!" Esther thought, and she wondered why she hadn't remembered it before. "The spirit has been praying for me all of this time."

Esther felt like a heavy weight had been lifted from her shoulders. People didn't need her to do their praying for them. They just needed to know what Paul had revealed long ago, and what the Saints of every age have discovered in their "dark nights of the soul": We are never utterly alone. Even when we cannot bring ourselves to pray, when no words come to describe what we are thinking and feeling, the Spirit prays for us.

At last Esther's heart was filled with peace. For the first time in many weeks she was able to go back to sleep and to sleep soundly until morning. This time when she dreamed, she walked into the cave and wandered from room to room, lingering in some longer than others, allowing herself to come in touch with all of the beauty that God had placed within her soul. She awoke refreshed and full of the Spirit.

The following Sunday in worship Esther stood during the time for sharing joys and prayer concerns. She told us about her dream and the peace that came to her when she listened to what God was telling her in the dream. She said, "I will no longer be your 'town-pray-er' but," she added, "I will be very glad to take my turn whenever there is a need for someone to lead in prayer.''

It may have been my imagination, but I thought I heard the pastor heave a great sigh of relief.

A Happy Mother's Day

Her children rise up and call her blessed.
                                                    Proverbs 31:28

There was once an old woman by the name of Mrs. Simpson who lived all alone in a big, green house on the end of a quiet street in a small American city. Mrs. Simpson was known to the children in her neighborhood as the flowers-and-cookies lady. She loved to tend the flowers in her yard and she always had cookies for the children when they stopped to visit on their way home from school.

One Mother's Day Mrs. Simpson found herself feeling rather lonely. Her children were all grown and lived in distant places. They sent cards and they phoned, but they lived too far away to visit. How sad, she thought, not to see one's children on Mother's Day.

And then something wonderful happened. The doorbell rang. When she opened the door, there were all the children of the neighborhood. "Happy Mother's Day," they all chimed together. "We love you Mrs. Simpson!" And then the youngest child sang out alone, "We have a surprise for you." She took her hand from behind her back and held out a big bouquet of dandelions. Mrs. Simpson gave her a big hug. Then she hugged each of the children in turn and insisted that they all come inside for some milk and cookies.

When the children had gone, Mrs. Simpson thought to herself that this had been one of the nicest Mother's Days she had ever had.

Author's Note: *This story is dedicated to my Mom, Bernice Lois Long Sumwalt and to my Grandmother, Leona Amanda Long.*

Memorial Day Miracle

Hearken to me, you who pursue deliverance, you who seek the Lord; look to the rock from which you were hewn, and to the quarry from which you were digged.

Isaiah 51:1

Brian and his two good friends, Pete and Dave, had a peculiar hobby. On warm spring nights when the moon was full they liked to go to the cemetery and tip over tombstones. They thought it was great fun. They figured the dead wouldn't know the difference, and the fact that it upset the grown-ups so much made it all the more fun.

One night, just before Memorial Day, they went to the cemetery to look for just the right tombstone to tip. Each time they tried to find one that was bigger and harder to topple than the one before. They looked through the whole cemetery and when they came to the old section they saw the perfect stone. It was about six feet tall with a cross on top and a pot of geraniums on each side. The inscription was so worn they could barely read it. It said something about an Alfred Coggens who died in 1917.

It took all of them a good ten minutes of pushing and pulling before they finally tipped it over. When they were finished, they all laughed and congratulated themselves on the fine prank they had pulled.

The next day Brian's Grandpa Ernie stopped by their house on his way to the cemetery. He wanted to know if they would all like to go with him. Brian's Dad said, "Sure." So they all hopped in the car with Grandpa and headed for the cemetery. Brian didn't really want to go, of course, but he thought he had better keep quiet lest they suspect something.

When they arrived at the cemetery Brian was surprised at how nice it looked. He had never seen the cemetery in the daylight. There were flowers and potted plants everywhere. But what struck Brian most were the small American flags waving in the breeze. He asked his Dad what they were for. His Dad said they were placed over the graves of veteran soldiers who had fought in the country's wars as a way of honoring them for their service.

Grandpa Ernie took them on a tour of the cemetery. He pointed out the graves of people he had known and told stories about those who had been his good friends. It seemed that Grandpa had a lot of friends in the cemetery.

By this time Brian was starting to get nervous. And when they came to the old part of the cemetery, he was downright petrified. What would Grandpa say when he saw the stone he and his friends had tipped over? Would he be able to tell who had done it? Brian was sure his face would give him away.

At last they came to Alfred Coggens' old stone. And when he saw it, Brian could hardly believe his eyes. It was standing straight and tall just as it had been the night before. The two potted geraniums were back in their places and there was a small American flag waving between them. Brian stood and stared in disbelief.

There was fresh sand at the base of the stone, but no one noticed. Everyone was watching Grandpa Ernie. When he came to the stone he stopped, stood at attention and saluted. Then after a long, lingering silence he told them about Alfred Coggens.

Alfred had been Grandpa's best friend. They had fought together in France during World War I. Grandpa talked quietly and sadly about the war of the trenches, the barbed wire, the poison gas, and the hundreds of men he watched die from bullets and exploding shells. He had a far away look in his eyes as he told how he and Alfred had been trapped behind enemy lines. He was wounded by shell fragments in both legs. Alfred had carried him 400 yards back to their trench. Just as they reached safety, Alfred had been struck and killed by an enemy bullet.

By this time Brian was feeling deeply ashamed of what he and his friends had done. And when he thought of Grandpa fighting in that awful war and Alfred saving his life, his eyes filled with tears. He looked at Grandpa Ernie and said, "If it hadn't been for Alfred, you might not be here, and then Dad wouldn't be here and I wouldn't be here either."

"That's right," said Grandpa, "I'm glad you understand. Many people have forgotten."

"I'll never forget," said Brian. And he never did.

Brian is grown now and has a son and daughter of his own. And every Memorial Day he takes them to the cemetery and tells them the story of Alfred Coggens and the once toppled stone.

Author's Note: *(Isaiah 51:1-6 is not the lectionary text of the day. The story is shared here as one possible resource for Memorial Day.)*

Children of God

So then, brethren, we are debtors, not to the flesh, to live according to the flesh — for if you live according to the flesh you will die, but if by the Spirit you put to death the deeds of the body you will live. For all who are led by the Spirit of God are sons of God. For you did not receive the spirit of slavery to fall back into fear, but you have received the spirit of sonship. When we cry, "Abba! Father!" it is the Spirit himself bearing witness with our spirit that we are children of God, and if children, then heirs, heirs of God and fellow heirs with Christ, provided we suffer with him in order that we may also be glorified with him.

Romans 8:12-17

Once upon a time there was a very old woman who lived on the edge of a small town in a big white frame house. The house looked quite run down because the woman was becoming too weak to take care of it. The paint was peeling off the boards, and some of the windows were cracked. The grass had grown high on the lawn, the picket fence was falling down and the bushes were overgrown and thick. The old woman tried to maintain it all, but it was just more than she could do.

She was a good woman. She had provided a good home for her family, she worked hard in her community and in her church, but now she was gettting so old that she barely had enough strength to go to the store for groceries. And she was all alone. Her husband had died a few years before at the age of ninety-three. Her two sons had been killed in the war and her daughter had died of cancer at an early age.

All the woman had left was a little dog name Bertie, after the Prince of Wales whom she had heard stories about as a little girl. Bertie had been with her for years and years. In dog years, he was almost as old as she was. How she loved that dog. She called him her "little boy," and she spoiled him with generous portions of leftovers from her own plate. Whatever she ate, Bertie ate, too. And when she had a chocolate candy after supper, Bertie always got one, too.

Bertie and the old woman were inseparable. They did everything, and went everywhere, together.

One day, while Bertie was playing out on the front lawn chasing gophers, and the old woman was trying to wash the windows on the front porch, a group of boys came along and snatched Bertie before the old woman knew what was happening. They tied a rope around his neck and dragged him along behind their bicycles. They thought it was good fun, and they brought him home after only two trips around the block. They hadn't meant any harm, but it was all too much for Bertie. He died of exhaustion a few hours later.

The old woman was heartbroken, but she made up her mind that she wouldn't let it get her down. She had gone through too much for that. She called up the boys' parents, most of whom had been through her Sunday School class years before when she taught sixth grade in the church school — and she bawled them out. She scolded them over the phone. She said, "If you paid more attention to those boys they wouldn't get into trouble like this. And furthermore, if you would take them to church every Sunday, instead of once in awhile when you feel like it, they might know the difference between right and wrong." She went on and on. And when she was finished, she said, "I want you to send those boys over to my place right now so I can talk to them."

They all came, and you never saw a more frightened lot. The old woman met them at the door, ushered them in, and sat them down around the dining room table. The boys expected her to shout at them and tell them how bad they were. But, instead, the old woman served them hot chocolate and cookies. They weren't very hungry, because they were so scared, but they ate anyway because they were afraid not to.

Finally, when the cookies were all gone, the old woman got out her scrap book and showed them the pictures of her family and of her dear dog, Bertie. By this time the boys were beginning to feel ashamed. They asked her what they could do to make up for the terrible thing they had done.

The old woman said, "There is nothing you can do. I know you won't do it again. But I would be very pleased if you would come and eat cookies with me once in awhile." They all agreed that they would come.

After they were gone, the old woman thought, "Something good may come out of this, after all." She still missed Bertie very much, but not long after that she went down to the humane society and found a little dog about the same size as Bertie. She decided to call him Charlie, after the current Prince of Wales. It was not the same as having Bertie back, but she grew to love him just the same.

As for the boys, they kept their promise. They came every week for cookies. Some of them stopped by more often. In time she let them help her do the things she wasn't able to do for herself. They fixed up the fence, mowed the lawn, trimmed the bushes, painted the house and replaced the cracked windows. The old woman and the boys became fast friends. They called her Grandma, and she loved them as if they were her own.

Willy Who?

*. . . the Lord sees not as man sees; man looks on
the outward appearance, but the Lord looks on the
heart.*

1 Samuel 16:7b

Once upon a time there was a mixed-up boy named Willy.
Willy wasn't sure how he felt about himself. Sometimes he
liked himself and thought that he was really an all right guy.
At other times he thought he was the dumbest, slowest, ugli-
est, wimpiest, no-talent kid in the world.

Willy had different names for himself depending on how
he was feeling and how his day was going.

When he wore his Chicago Cubs baseball cap backwards
with his Mickey Mouse T-shirt, his hot pink shades, and the
red and green socks his Aunt Edith gave him for Christmas,
and the kids at school all laughed at him, he thought of himself as Weird Willy.

When he was on the baseball field and he saw his favorite
pitch coming, a fast ball about knee high, and he hit it over
the fence for a home run and the kids all cheered, he thought
of himself as Wow Willy.

When his Mom and Dad got divorced and they had to live
in separate houses and he had to take turns staying with each
of them and he was afraid that it might have been partly his
fault, he felt very, very small. Wee Willy, that was him, so
tiny he might disappear altogether.

When his girlfriend, Gertrude, came over on Friday nights
to watch television and snuggled up next to him on the living
room couch, told him how strong and handsome he was, and
sometimes kissed him on the ear during the commercials, he
felt like he was ten feet tall. Then he thought of himself as
Wonderful Willy.

104

When his big brothers were around, there was always a wrestling match or a race or a tug of war or just plain pushing and shoving and Willy always lost. He couldn't do anything as well as his big brothers did. At least that's the way he felt. It was then that he thought of himself as Wimpy Willy.

But when he was in science class at school, where Mr. Enright, his favorite teacher, taught, he always felt good about himself. Mr. Enright said he was a good student because he was always asking questions and looking for the answers. In science class he was Why Willy The Whiz Kid. Mr. Enright said he would make a good scientist someday.

One day Willy was playing basketball on the playground with some of the big junior high kids. While he was dribbling for a lay-up, one of the big boys stuck out his foot and tripped him. Willy fell down on the asphalt and skinned his knee. It hurt as bad as any hurt he had ever had. And he couldn't stop himself; he began to cry and cry. One of the boys pointed at him and called him Weepy Willy. Then all of the boys began to say it together: "Weepy, weepy, weepy Willy." When he continued to cry they called him a cry baby and told him to go home to his mother.

Willy felt as about as low as he had ever felt in his life. And he was beginning to wonder who he really was. Was he Weird Willy or Wow Willy or Wee Willy or Wonderful Willy or Why Willy The Whiz Kid or Weepy Willy the cry baby? Willy wasn't sure and he didn't know what to do.

He decided to stop by the science room and see Mr. Enright. Mr. Enright was preparing some experiments for the next day's classes. Willy told him how he was feeling and about all the different names he called himself. He asked Mr. Enright how he could know who he really was. Mr. Enright listened carefully and when Willy was finished he said:

(What do you think Mr. Enright said? What would you say to Willy?)

How To Forgive a Fallen Father

From now on, therefore, we regard no one from a human point of view; even though we once regarded Christ from a human point of view, we regard him thus no longer. Therefore, if any one is in Christ, he is a new creation; the old has passed away, behold, the new has come.

2 Corinthians 5:16-17

On the eve of his sixteenth birthday, Jimmy Morton's world fell apart. It started first thing in the morning, after he arrived at school. He stopped by his locker to pick up some books and, Alan Trammel poked his head around the corner, by the water fountain, and yelled, "Hey, Jimmy, guess who I saw your old man with last night? Helen Marcion!"

Helen Marcion had a reputation for hanging around bars and going out with a lot of men, anyone and everyone, or so people said.

"It looks like your pa is getting himself a little something on the side."

That did it for Jimmy. He tore down the hall, and began to pound Alan Trammel with both fists. Jimmy had never been so furious in his whole life. If someone hadn't pulled them apart, Alan might have been seriously injured.

As he headed for his first class, he felt ashamed of himself for reacting so violently. But then, Alan shouldn't have said what he said. His Dad might be a lot of things, and they might not get along sometimes, but he knew his Dad would never cheat on his Mom.

That night, on the way home from the football game, he stopped off at the drive-in to get an ice cream cone. On the way out, he happened to look into the parking lot across the street, and he couldn't believe what he saw. He didn't want to believe what he saw. There was his Dad, coming out of a motel room with Helen Marcion. He ducked down behind a car so they wouldn't see him.

On the way home, he felt sick inside, scared sick, the kind of sick you feel when your life is on the line or when it seems that everything you hold dear in life is about to be lost.

When he got home, Jimmy went straight to bed. He didn't sleep much that night. And the next morning, at breakfast when his Dad said Happy Birthday, he couldn't bring himself to look at him, let alone speak to him.

After his Mom left for work, Jimmy's Dad asked him what was the matter. Jimmy didn't say anything. Finally in utter frustration, his Dad said, "Well, be that way then, but when I get home tonight, I want some kind of explanation."

Then Jimmy couldn't stop himself. He just let it pour out. "You don't have any right to tell me anything. I saw you out with Helen Marcion last night!"

Without warning his Dad slapped him hard across the face. And then he left. He just picked up his dinner pail and walked out the door.

That was the beginning of a long, awful silence between them. Jimmy's Mom tried to get them to talk, even that first night at his birthday supper, but neither one would say a word. It was the unhappiest birthday Jimmy had ever had.

It went on like that for several weeks. Jimmy was determined that he was never going to speak to his Dad again. He was so angry and so hurt that he just wanted to run away and start over again. But there was nowhere to go and it seemed like there was no way for the awful nightmare to end.

One day during English class, Jimmy got a message to report to the office. When he got there the principal told him his father had been in an accident at work, and his mother called him to say he should come to the hospital immediately. The principal offered to drive him.

Jimmy had that scared sick feeling in his stomach all the way to the hospital. They went directly to the emergency room waiting area, where his mother, his grandpa and grandma, his mother's brother, Uncle Ben, the minister and a couple of their close neighbors were already gathered.

Jimmy could tell from the looks on their faces that his father was seriously hurt. They said a scaffolding had collapsed throwing him twenty feet to a concrete floor. There were numerous broken bones, but the biggest concern was a skull fracture and the possibility of damage to his spinal cord. The doctors were working to stabilize him before taking him to surgery.

When the doctor came out, about a half hour later, he said Mr. Morton was stable but would require immediate surgery to repair some damaged blood vessels in his brain. He said the operation was risky, but he had only a 50/50 chance of survival if they didn't operate. He said he was conscious and wanted to talk to his wife and son before the surgery.

Suddenly Jimmy felt a big knot in the pit of his stomach. He got up and ran out of the room. He found a bench outside and as he sat down he just couldn't help himself, he began to cry. Why does life have to be so complicated, he thought? Why can't it be like it used to be? Why did his father have to do what he did?

After a little bit Jimmy felt a hand on his shoulder. It was his Uncle Ben. Jimmy had always been close to Uncle Ben. He was only about ten years older than Jimmy and it seemed like they could always talk.

He told his uncle everything that had happened, how awful he was feeling, and how he didn't know if he could face his father, even though he might be dying. "What am I going to do, Uncle Ben?"

Uncle Ben didn't say anything for a long time. He just sat there with his arm around Jimmy's shoulder. Finally, he said, "You love your father very much, don't you, Jimmy? That's why you feel so angry about what he did. You wouldn't feel that way if you didn't love him." Jimmy nodded.

"Now, let me ask you this," his uncle said, "does one mistake, even though it is a serious one, wipe out all of those years of love?"

That did it. Jimmy hugged his uncle and ran back into the hospital. His mom was just coming out of his father's room. He hugged her, but they didn't speak. She just nodded that he should go in.

As he drew near the bed, his father smiled at him, took his hand, and squeezed it. Before he could say anything, his father said, "Jimmy, I know you're angry with me, and you have a right to be. I am not going to try to explain why I did what I did. I'm not even sure I know myself. But I know this. I love your mother and I love you more than anything else in the world. I want you always to remember that."

In that moment Jimmy felt whole again. He was still scared about the operation, but he knew that, whatever happened, at least things were right between him and his dad.

He squeezed his father's hand and said, "I love you, too, Dad."

The Day of Salvation

All this is from God, who through Christ reconciled us to himself and gave us the ministry of reconciliation . . .

. . . For he says, "At the acceptable time I have listened to you, and helped you on the day of salvation." Behold, now is the acceptable time; behold, now is the day of salvation.

2 Corinthians 5:18 & 6:2

There were once two families who lived side by side on the same street. The two men worked for the same company and rode to work together in the neighborhood car pool. The two women worked in different buildings downtown but always managed to meet for lunch in the middle of the week. Their children played together, they shared lawn tools and loaned each other sugar and eggs. In the warm months they barbecued, boated and camped together. During the school year there were long conversations over coffee after chauffering the kids to basketball games and school dances. They were the best of friends. They shared their hopes and dreams, their joys, their worries, their heartaches and their disappointments. And when they worshiped together in the same church on Sunday mornings, each one gave thanks for their wonderful friends.

Then one day something happened at church which brought an end to their friendship. No one remembers the details of the incident. It may have been something the pastor did, or something someone said at a meeting. It all came to a head in a shouting argument in the fellowship hall one Sunday after a potluck dinner. Neither family was directly involved in the dispute, but it was such an unseemly scene that both of them swore they would never go back.

110

Several people from the church, including the pastor, came to visit to try to persuade them to change their minds. One man even came to apologize and one of the families did change their minds. They decided that the church meant too much to them to let a difference of opinion and a few unkind words keep them away.

But the other family never went back. They said, "If that's the way the church is going to be, we want no part of it."

From that time on, the two families began to drift further and further apart. There were no more backyard barbecues, no sharing of tools or feelings, and no more midweek lunches for the wives. The men still rode to work together, but it was only out of convenience.

The family who stayed with the church became more involved than ever before. The children were active in Sunday School. Mom and Dad served on various committees and eventually became lay leaders of the church. They were the family everyone looked to for leadership and support. No one in the church worked harder, loved more, or was more loved.

The other family never found another church. They talked about it. They almost went looking on a couple of occasions, but just couldn't bring themselves to go. Deep down they were afraid that all churches were alike, so they looked elsewhere for a sense of community. They became more active in civic organizations, they joined the Y and a community singing group. They made many new friends; they were busier than they had ever been before. They told themselves they didn't need the church. They could do good and serve God just as well, perhaps even better, without the church.

Then one day there was a terrible accident while the two neighbor men were on their way to work. Both men were critically injured. Their wives were called from work, the children came from school, and the two families who were almost strangers now sat across from each other in the intensive care waiting room. The church family was surrounded by people from the congregation. The pastor was there and several of their friends. They prayed together and clung to each other as they waited.

The other family sat alone. The woman hadn't known who to call, and if any of their friends had heard the news, none of them came to sit with them in their hour of need.

Finally, after some time had passed, and during one of the long silences which ensue in a room like that after everything has been said and there's nothing to do but wait, the woman from the church got up, went across the room to her old friend, put her arms around her and through her tears said, "I need you. I don't think I can get through this without you."

Her friend said, "I need you, too. I was afraid you didn't need me." They embraced and then they sat and waited together.

When the doctor came out it was with a sorrowful step. The man from the church had died. The other man would live, but he would never be able to walk again.

Somehow the two families got through the funeral and the long weeks of hospitalization and rehabilitation. And on the very first Sunday morning after the surviving neighbor came home from the hospital, they all went to worship together. He and his family were warmly welcomed by the congregation. And after a time he and his wife became lay leaders in the church. As the years passed they made up for the time they had lost. They were tireless witnesses. Every Monday morning they would call the pastor and ask for a list of persons who were in need of the church's ministry. And then they would go from door to door and tell their story to everyone who would listen. They became what Paul called, 'ambassadors for Christ," sharing with all the message of reconciliation that had been entrusted to them.

The Sleeping Giant

And if any place will not receive you and they refuse to hear you, when you leave shake off the dust that is on your feet for a testimony against them.
                                        Mark 6:11

Long ago in a distant mountain village there lived a God-fearing people who had fallen on hard times. The village had once been prosperous and full of life, but now the people were very poor and beginning to lose hope. They longed for a miracle, some sign that God had not forgotten them.

Late one Saturday evening a very sleepy giant stumbled into the village square. And as there was no one about he simply lay his head down on the church steps and went to sleep.

The next morning when it came time to worship, God's people didn't know what to do. Everyone came to the church at the appointed hour, but no one was able to enter. Just as people began to give up hope and drift away toward their homes, someone said, "Why don't we go in through the back door?" Everyone tiptoed around the giant and went in through the back door of the church.

The service began on time, as usual. The people sang and prayed, the scripture was read, the preacher preached, the offering was brought to the altar and no mention was made of the giant.

Years passed and every Sunday was the same. The giant continued to sleep on the church steps. God's people came to worship at the appointed hour, always tiptoeing around the giant and entering through the back door of the church. The service always began on time. The people sang and prayed, the scripture was read, the preacher preached, the offering was brought to the altar, and no mention was made of the giant.

One Sunday morning a stranger appeared at the door of the church. She was very old and she walked slowly with the aid of a gnarled cane. When she discovered that the front door was blocked, she walked up to the giant's head, pulled herself up to her full height and whispered something in the giant's ear. Suddenly the giant snorted in his sleep and shifted his head leaving a clear path to the door. The old woman climbed up the steps, opened the door, walked into the sanctuary and sat down on the very last bench in the back.

Everyone else tiptoed around the giant and entered through the back door of the church as usual. The service began on time. The people sang and prayed, the scripture was read, the preacher preached, the offering was brought to the altar and, as usual, no mention was made of the giant.

Just as the preacher was about to pronounce the benediction, the old woman stood up and said in a loud voice, "Why don't you wake up the giant?"

God's people sat in stunned silence. No one moved or breathed for more than a minute.

The old woman repeated the question, this time in a soft pleading voice, "Why don't you wake up the giant?"

The silence continued for a long time. At last a small child spoke up. "We must never wake up the giant. He might kill us, and if he didn't kill us, he would surely eat us out of house and home."

The old woman waited. No one else ventured to speak. "Very well," she said, "I shall take the giant with me." She turned and walked out the same door through which she had entered. God's people got up and went out through the back door of the church as usual, tiptoed around the giant and watched in amazement as the old woman raised her cane and shouted, "God's will be done!"

The giant woke up with a start, climbed slowly to his feet, stretched his legs, offered his hand to the old woman, and the two of them walked off together. When they reached the edge of the village, they paused and shook the dust from their feet. Then without so much as a single glance at those who were watching, they turned their backs on the village and went deliberately on their way.

The next Sunday morning God's people came to worship at the appointed hour, tiptoed around, and entered through the back door of the church as usual, except for one small child, the one who spoke up when the old woman asked the question. The child entered through the front door of the church and sat down on the very last bench in the back.

The service began on time. The people sang and prayed, the scripture was read, the preacher preached, the offering was brought to the altar and, as usual, no mention was made of the giant.

Just as the preacher was about to give the benediction, the small child stood up and said in a soft pleading voice, "Why don't we wake up the giant?"

A Corn-fed Beef

And do not grieve the Holy Spirit of God, in whom you were sealed for the day of redemption. Let all bitterness and wrath and anger and clamor and slander be put away from you, with all malice, and be kind to one another, tenderhearted, forgiving one another, as God in Christ forgave you.

Ephesians 4:30-32

So if you are offering your gift at the altar, and there remember that your brother has something against you, leave your gift at the altar and go; first be reconciled to your brother, and then come and offer your gift.

Matthew 5:23-24

There were once two farmers who were bitter rivals. The two had once been fast friends. They had fished and hunted together as boys. In high school both had been stars on the football and basketball teams. When they married, each took his turn as best man at the other's wedding. On Friday nights they went out with their wives for fish and dancing at the local supper club. Both served as leaders in their little country church. Their adjoining farms were the pride of the county. The two men were admired and loved by all.

And then one year one of the seed corn companies offered a new tractor to the farmer who could grow the most corn per acre on a designated forty acre test plot. Almost every farmer in the county entered the contest but everyone knew that in the end it would come down to Jake and Burt. They always had the highest yields.

The corn was planted, summer came and the weather was perfect, just enough rain and hot humid days to make the corn grow tall and green. It was going to be a good year.

As harvest time approached, Jake walked down through his test field one day, paced off a hundred yards, and counted the ears on one of the rows. There were a good many stalks with double ears, some with three, but he wasn't sure if it would be enough. When he came to the edge of the field, he looked around to see if anyone was watching; seeing no one he climbed over the fence into Burt's test field, picked a row at random, paced off a hundred yards and counted the ears. His fears were confirmed. It appeared that Burt's yield was going to run about ten percent ahead of his own.

This bothered Jake a good deal. It seemed to him that Burt was always just a little bit better. When they were in high school, Burt had been captain of the football team, most valuable player on the basketball team and homecoming king two years in a row. After graduation it was Burt who was chosen Young Farmer of the Year first. He had been chosen the year after, but Burt was always first. And now Burt was going to be first again.

Something happened in Jake. He didn't know what came over him, but one night on the way home from a church meeting, chaired by Burt, he went around by the back road, stopped the pickup along side of Burt's test field, reached down and took a pair of wire cutters out of the tool box under the seat. Burt's test field was next to a pasture where he ran about a hundred head of beef cattle. Jake stepped over to the fence and snipped the four taut wires that protected the corn from the cattle.

There was no contest after that. Jake won the new tractor easily with about fifteen bushels per acre more than the second place finisher. Burt never said anything publicly against Jake because he had no proof, but he knew in his heart what had happened. He hardly spoke to Jake after that except to be polite when they came across each other at the store or on Sunday mornings in church. For thirty years they lived side by side, sat across the aisle from each other on different sides of the church, barely speaking or in any other way acknowledging what had once been between them. The whole community felt the tension which they carried with them wherever they went.

Then one day word got around that Jake had colon cancer. Burt was deeply disturbed when he heard the news. It bothered him that one of them might die before they had made their peace.

That Sunday when the pastor gave the invitation to come forward for Holy Communion, Burt stepped across the aisle to Jake, put his arms on his shoulders, looked him in the eye and said, "All of these years I have been angry with you. I want to let it go. Will you forgive me?" Jake put his arms around Burt and the two men held on to each other for over a minute. Tears filled their eyes as the anger and bitterness of thirty years melted away. Everyone in the congregation breathed a great sigh of relief. The tension was gone.

The next morning when Burt went out to do his chores he found a shiny new tractor parked in the driveway. Attached to the steering wheel was a note which read, "Let's go fishing. Your friend, Jake."

The Boy Who Had Everything

*I am the living bread which came down from heaven;
if anyone eats of this bread, he will live forever; and
the bread which I shall give for the life of the world
is my flesh.*

John 6:51

There was once a boy who had everything. At least he thought he had everything. He lived in a big, beautiful house, with a swimming pool and a tree house in the backyard. He had a ten-speed bike, a go-cart and an all-terrain vehicle in the garage, all of which he could ride any time he pleased. In his room he had a television, a VCR, a stereo, a compact disc player, a computer, a Nintendo and dozens of video games. He even had his own telephone and answering machine.

On Saturday and Sunday mornings, the boy who had everything played with all of his wonderful things. Sometimes he and his Dad would go biking or ride their all-terrain vehicles down at the beach. In the afternoons he went shopping with his Mom and Dad at the mall and they bought more wonderful things. Somehow it never seemed to be enough. He had a hunger, deep down inside himself, for something else. He wasn't sure what it was that he was hungry for, but he knew it was something he didn't have.

The boy who lived next door to the boy who had everything didn't have nearly as many nice things. He lived in a modest house with a small backyard which had barely enough room for his tire-swing and sandbox. He had a three-speed bike and a red wagon in his garage, and in his room there was a cage with his pet hamster, his baseball card collection, his comic books and a wall covered with posters. He also had a dog named Rex who knew how to roll over and play dead.

119

On Saturdays the boy next door played catch with his Dad in the backyard. In the afternoon, sometimes, his Mom would fix a picnic supper, and they would go to the park or fishing at the lake. On Sundays they all went to church.

The boy who had everything had noticed that the boy next door went to church on Sundays with his parents. He asked his Mom and Dad about it, and they said that church was fine for some people, but it wasn't for them.

One Sunday morning, the boy who had everything was playing up in his treehouse, when he noticed the boy next door getting into the car with his parents. They were all dressed up in their best clothes. He watched as they drove away and when the car was just about out of sight, he hopped on his ten-speed bike and followed them for several blocks down the street and around the corner to their church. He watched from behind a tree as they got out of the car and went into the building. There were a great many other children going into the church with their parents, too. After everyone had gone in, and he could hear music coming from the organ inside the church, he decided that maybe it would be all right if he went in very quietly to see what it was that went on in church.

He tiptoed in. A door was open to a big room where all the people were seated on long benches. He stood behind the door post and watched and listened as the people sang songs and a man dressed in a white robe and standing on what looked like a little stage with a big podium, read from a large leather-bound book. Then the man closed the book and talked for a little while. After that he invited everyone to give something he called their offerings. Several people went around with little gold bowls to get all of the offerings. It appeared to him that people were putting money in the bowls. When they were finished they took the bowls up to a table in the center of the stage. The man in the white robe went over and uncovered a vase and a loaf of bread. He said some words and then he invited everyone to come up and eat. The little boy was surprised to see that people knelt down before they ate. Watching all of this made him very hungry and he hoped that they would offer him some of the bread, too.

When everyone was finished the man in the white robe held up the vase and the bread and asked, "Is there anyone else who would like to come?"

The boy didn't know what came over him, he couldn't help himself; he stepped out from behind the door post and called out, "Yes, I would like to come. May I have some?"

The man in the white robe said, "Why of course you may have some. It is especially for you."

The boy who had everything went forward and knelt down in front of the man in the white robe. The man broke off a big piece of the bread and showed the little boy how to dip it in a dark colored liquid in the vase. When he put it in his mouth it tasted sweet and satisfying like nothing he had ever tasted before. In that moment the little boy knew that now he truly had everything he would ever need.

Help Me Get Home

And he took a child, and put him in the midst of them; and taking him in his arms he said to them, "Whoever receives one such child in my name receives me; and whoever receives me, receives not me but him who sent me."

Mark 9:36-37

There was once a little boy about ten years old who lived in a grand old house on the edge of the business district in a small city. The house had a big front yard and an even bigger backyard which ran all the way down to the river. It was a setting which promised endless opportunities for little boys.

But, alas, not for this one, because he was never at home. Home didn't mean anything special to him. It was only a big empty house and big vacant yard. There was no one there who cared if he was there. In fact, he had a feeling down deep inside, so deep that he rarely noticed it, and so deep that if you asked him about it, he would have denied it, a feeling that no one cared about him at all. So he was never at home. He was always uptown looking for something.

He had a daily routine. First he would check the pay phones for change, then he hit the laundromat and all the pop machines and newspaper stands in front of the stores on Main Street. He always picked up a quarter or two. Then it was off to the bars. He could usually find a drunk who would give him a dime toward a candy bar or a bag of potato chips. Sometimes, not every day lest he wear out his welcome, he would run into the stores and cause such a commotion that the storekeepers would give him a pack of gum or a roll of Life Savers just so he would go away. And so he would go hang around on the street corners, and hang over the railing on the bridge, and sit in the doorways and watch people go by.

Long after the stores were closed and most people had gone home for supper, he would still be there, barefooted, shirtless, in the same frayed cutoffs he wore every day, peering around corners, peeking into windows, looking — for what he didn't know. He only knew it was something he didn't have. And he had a vague suspicion it was something he had a right to have because it seemed like everyone else had it.

One Sunday morning while everyone was in church singing the glories of God out of the hymnal, and the little boy was looking and watching in his usual places, he was suddenly overwhelmed by an impulse which he couldn't deny. He reached down into the gutter and picked up a stone. And in utter frustration, in the anger and the hurt and the longing which had welled up for so long in the deep recesses of his heart, he threw it — through the stained glass window of the church.

The congregation stopped singing in mid-verse; the organist stopped playing; the minister looked up from his notes; one of the ushers went to get a broom; the chairman of the Trustees calculated [in his head] how much it would cost to replace the window, and somewhere in the back of the church one of the little babies began to cry. Everyone else sat in stunned silence. Who would do such a thing? On Sunday morning? During church?

Through the shards of broken glass some of those sitting near the window could see who had thrown the stone. "It's a little kid. It's that Burlson kid. Ohhh!" Ripples of "Ohs" went up and down the pews. Now everybody knew.

The minister didn't know what to do, so he did what he always did when he didn't know what to do. He asked the congregation. "What shall we do?"

Some wanted to call the police. Others said, "Call his parents."

"No," someone said, "you know they're never home."

One man suggested writing a letter to the City Council. He said, "There should be an ordinance to keep kids like that off the streets."

Another man stood up and said, "Well, we've got to do something. We can't have kids throwing rocks through our stained glass windows. It won't be safe to come to church. For all we know he may throw another one in here at any moment."

Everyone ducked their heads and sank down a little lower in their pews.

"I vote we go catch him right now and tan his little hide." There was a murmur of approval from the crowd.

"Yeah, that's what we should do. Let's go get him."

"Why don't we just go talk to him?" It was old Mrs. Aikers from the retirement apartment building up the street. "Why don't we just go talk to him and see what he wants."

Suddenly it became very quiet in the church. All eyes were on Mrs. Aikers as she climbed slowly to her feet, hanging tightly onto her cane. "Maybe he just needs someone to talk to," she said. "I'll go talk to him."

Everyone watched in silence as the old woman made her way with some difficulty to the back of the church. They were more stunned than when the stone came through the window. Mrs. Aikers was the last person anyone expected to do anything about anything! No one even helped her out the door.

They heard her, though, through the hole in the broken window. "Jerry," she said, "come here, I want you to help me get home."

The very next morning the chairman of the Trustees got a call. It was old Mrs. Aikers. "Frank," she said, "I want you to get that window fixed. Can you do it by Sunday?"

"We'll do our best," he told her.

"And by the way," she said, "I'd appreciate it if you'd send me the bill."

The next Sunday they were back in church together — old Mrs. Aikers and Jerry Burlson sitting side by side in the very spot where the stone came through the window.

The Rich Young Squirrel

And as he was setting out on his journey, a man ran up and knelt before him, and asked him, "Good Teacher, what must I do to inherit eternal life?" And Jesus said to him, "Why do you call me good? No one is good but God alone. You know the commandments: Do not kill, Do not commit adultery, Do not steal, Do not bear false witness, Do not defraud, Honor your father and mother," And he said to him, "Teacher, all these I have observed from my youth." And Jesus looking upon him loved him, and said to him, "You lack one thing; go, sell what you have, and give to the poor, and you will have treasure in heaven; and come follow me." At that saying his countenance fell, and he went away sorrowful; for he had great possessions.

Mark 10:17-22
(See also Matthew 19:16-30 and Luke 18:18-30)

Once upon a time there was a rich young squirrel. He became rich by getting up early every morning before all of the other squirrels. In a short time he had more nuts than any other squirrel in the forest. In fact, he had more nuts than he could ever eat. He had nuts in the cupboard, nuts in the refrigerator, nuts in the sink and nuts under the table. He even had nuts in the bathtub. He had so many nuts that there was hardly any room for him to move around in his nest.

But, he wasn't happy. In fact, he was miserable. He had discovered that there is more to life than having all the nuts you want to eat.

One day a wise teacher-squirrel came to town. The rich young squirrel went to see him, and when he found him he asked him, "Teacher, what must I do to live forever?" The teacher squirrel replied, you know what is written in the holy book: "Love God and love your neighbor as yourself." The rich young squirrel said, "I have done both these things, and I am still miserable. What else can I do?" The wise teacher squirrel said, "There is one more thing you must do. Gather up all your nuts and give them to the poor squirrels." When the rich young squirrel heard this he hung his head and walked away. He couldn't bear to give up all of his nuts, even though they were making him miserable.

If you were the rich young squirrel, what would you do?

Temptation

For we have not a high priest who is unable to sympathize with our weaknesses, but one who in every respect has been tempted as we are, yet without sinning. Let us then with confidence draw near to the throne of grace, that we may receive mercy and find grace to help in time of need.

Hebrews 4:15-16

So when the woman saw that the tree was good for food, and that it was a delight to the eyes, and that the tree was to be desired to make one wise, she took of its fruit and ate; and she also gave some to her husband and he ate.

Genesis 3:6

There were once two brothers who came face to face with temptation in the form of the proverbial apple. Their names were Leroy and Earl and they had an apple tree in their backyard that had the biggest, reddest, most delicious apples anyone had ever seen or tasted, that is if you waited for them to get ripe. Their mom had told them again and again that they were never to eat the apples while they were green. They could pick berries and tomatoes, cucumbers and radishes, almost anything else in the garden, but they were not to pick the apples until harvest time.

All summer, Leroy and Earl watched the little green apples grow bigger and bigger as each day passed. By the end of August, they were starting to turn red but they were still mostly green.

One day a group of kids from the neighborhood came over to play in the backyard. They spotted the almost ripe apples immediately, and one of them shouted, "Let's taste the apples!" She climbed up in the tree and before Leroy and Earl could say anything, she started picking apples and tossing them down to the other kids.

Finally, Earl shouted out, "We're not supposed to eat those apples till they ripen." But it was too late. They were already taking big bites. Leroy was eating one too.

"Come on," said Leroy, "have a bite. Mom won't mind if we eat just one. See how red they are?"

(Now, Earl has a decision to make. What do you think he should do?)

Unfortunately, that's not what he did. He couldn't resist. The apples looked so tasty, and after all, everyone else was eating one. So he ate one, too.

And do you know what happened? All of the kids who ate the green apples got stomach aches. And when Leroy and Earl's mother found out that they had eaten the forbidden fruit, they were grounded with no television and no video games, for three days.

A Distant Triumph Song

Then I saw a new heaven and a new earth; for the first heaven and the first earth had passed away, and the sea was no more. And I saw the holy city, new Jerusalem, coming down out of heaven from God, prepared as a bride adorned for her husband; and I heard a great voice from the throne saying, "Behold the dwelling place of God is with men. He will dwell with them and they shall be his people, and God himself will be with them; he will wipe away every tear from their eyes, and death shall be no more, neither shall there be mourning or crying or pain anymore, for the former things have passed away."

Revelation 21:1-4

After this I looked, and behold a great multitude which no man could number, from every nation, from all tribes and peoples and tongues, standing before the throne and before the Lamb, clothed in white robes with palm branches in their hands, and crying out with a loud voice, "Salvation belongs to our God who sits upon the throne and to the Lamb!"

Revelation 7:9-10

Therefore, since we are surrounded by so great a cloud of witnesses, let us also lay aside every weight, and sin which clings so closely and let us run with perseverance the race that is set before us, looking to Jesus the pioneer and perfector of our faith, who for the joy that was set before him endured the cross, despising the shame, and is seated at the right hand of the throne of God.

Hebrews 12:1-2

129

The Reverend Elizabeth Greer was tired. She found moving days exhausting and this day had been worse than most. The parsonage committee had not quite finished their papering and painting when the moving van arrived, so the movers put everything into one big pile in the middle of the living room. She managed to make the bedroom habitable with the help of some of the committee members, but everything else would have to wait. It was Saturday night and the next day would be her first Sunday in her new church. She was going over the sermon one last time when the phone rang. It was Anna Griswold. Elizabeth hadn't met Anna yet, but she had been told that she was one of the matriarchs of the church.

Anna said she hoped she wasn't calling at a bad time, and then she said, "If it isn't too late, some of the longtime members would like to get together with you for a while over at the church." It seemed like an odd request to Elizabeth since the church was planning a dinner and reception for her the next day after worship, but she was new after all, and she did want to make a good impression, so she said, "Certainly, I'll be glad to come."

"Good," said Anna. "How about 8:30 then, in the fellowship room?" Elizabeth said she would be there.

There were no cars in the parking lot, but the lights were on in the fellowship hall when Elizabeth arrived at the church. The building still felt very unfamiliar to her. She wondered what the people were like and if she would come to love them as she had loved the congregations she left behind at Hillside, Spring Creek and Woodley. They say your first charge is the hardest one to leave. Elizabeth had cried a good many tears when she said her final goodbyes there. It was hard to start over again. She wondered if she was up to it and if she would be needed and loved here as much as she was there.

Anna Griswold greeted her as she entered the hall. Elizabeth didn't know how she knew it was Anna, but as she took her hand she was aware of a warm feeling of familiarity. It felt almost as if she had known Anna all of her life. As the others came, she greeted them like old friends and called each one by name. And it didn't occur to her until long afterwards that she could not have known any of them until that night.

They took her to the center of the room where a table was covered with white linen and spread with ham sandwiches, baked beans, potato salad, jello in several different colors and shapes, pickles, olives, carrot sticks, radishes, celery, platters of thinly sliced cheeses and sausage, rolls, butter and a variety of cakes and pies, "a little lunch" Anna said, so they would have something to eat while they visited. They asked her to say the blessing, and then they all heaped their plates and sat down to eat.

By the time they were finished Elizabeth was full of food and good cheer. They shared memories and told stories about the saints of the church, those dear ones who had labored and loved here before them, and when their time came, had passed the work on to them. There was much laughter and more than a few mournful sighs as persons and events came to life through the telling and then slipped as quickly away when the stories were done.

It was almost midnight when Elizabeth locked the door and headed for home. The exhaustion she had felt earlier in the evening was gone. She felt strangely refreshed, at peace with herself and her new surroundings. She was going to like it here, and yes, they were going to like her, too.

The next morning when she greeted the congregation, Elizabeth was surprised to see that there were so few familiar faces among them. Where were all of those new friends she had come to know around that table downstairs the night before? It seemed odd that none of them were present to greet her on her first Sunday in the pulpit. And where was Anna?

When it came time for sharing joys and concerns a woman who appeared to be in her early sixties stood up and announced with some difficulty that her mother had died the night before. There was a murmuring of sorrowful "Ohs" from the congregation. Looking apologetically in Elizabeth's direction, the woman said that they had tried to call her but had been unable to reach her. Elizabeth thought to herself that it must have been while she was at the church.

131

Then she asked, "What was your mother's name?"

"Anna" the woman replied, "Anna Griswold." Elizabeth gripped the pulpit hard with both hands. She hoped she didn't appear as startled as she felt. "Anna?" she thought, "How could it be?"

Later that afternoon as she visited with the family in Anna's livingroom she learned that Anna had been bedridden for several years. But they said, "She was very excited about your coming and was looking forward to getting to know you."

"I feel like we do know each other," Elizabeth told them, but that was all she said. Nothing could have compelled her to say anything at all about her strange meeting at the church with Anna and the others the night before.

Everything went well at the funeral. It was a great celebration of Anna's life. She had been well loved and it was apparent that her witness had touched many lives. When they arrived at the cemetery, the words of William How's great hymn, "For All the Saints" were still running through Elizabeth's mind.

O blest communion, fellowship divine!
We feebly struggle, they in glory shine,

And when the strife is fierce, the warfare long
Steals on the ear the distant triumph song . . .

Her thoughts were interrupted as the funeral director let her out at the grave. Once again Elizabeth was strangely aware of a warm feeling of familiarity. She had never been to the cemetery before, but she recognized everything she saw. The names on the tombstones which surrounded the grave that had been opened for Anna were all familiar to her. She knew the faces and stories that went with everyone. Here they all were, those longtime members who had greeted her so warmly at that impromptu Saturday night reception. They were here where they belonged, their mortal remains in this familiar place and their spirits, shining somewhere in glory with the "countless host." It all made a weird kind of apocalyptic sense, like John's vision of the great multitude singing before the throne. How could she have expected them to be anywhere else?

132

It was the same at the luncheon after the burial. When all was ready, they asked her to say the blessing. Anna's daughter led her to the center of the fellowship hall where a table was covered with white linen and spread with him sandwiches, baked beans, potato salad, jello in several different colors and shapes, pickles, olives, carrot sticks, radishes, celery, platters of thinly sliced cheeses and sausage, rolls, butter, coffee and a variety of cakes and pies. Elizabeth had a sense that she had prayed over this table a hundred times before. She was where she belonged.

She whispered under her breath, "Thank you, Anna." Then she prayed aloud the words they expected to hear, and they all heaped their plates and sat down to eat, a blest communion, fellowship divine, their conversations accompanied by a faint, but unmistakable, distant triumph song.

Hondor and Subu

*And he sat down opposite the treasury, and watched
the multitude putting money into the treasury. Many
rich people put in large sums. And a poor widow
came, and put in two copper coins, which make a
penny. And he called his disciples to him, and said
to them, "Truly, I say to you, this poor widow has
put in more than all those who are contributing to
the treasury. For they all contributed out of their
abundance; but she out of her poverty has put in
everything she had, her whole living."*

Mark 12:41-44

*I do not mean that others should be eased and you
burdened, but that as a matter of equality your abundance at the present time should supply their want,
so that their abundance may supply your want, that
there may be equality. As it is written, "He who
gathered much had nothing over, and he who
gathered little had no lack."*

2 Corinthians 8:13-15

*All the tithe of the land, whether of the seed of the
land or of the fruit of the trees, is the LORD's; it
is holy to the LORD.*

Leviticus 27:30

There were once two squirrels named Hondor and Subu
(squirrels have strange names). Hondor and Subu were neighbors. They had grown up together and lived in the same little
town all of their lives. Subu's tree was just down the street
from Hondor's. Their kids played together in the mulberry

134

tree next to the bank. Hondor and Subu belonged to the Rotary Club and they were both members of Hickory Nut Community Church. They were not what one would call good friends but, they got along as neighbors do in small towns. They even helped each other, sometimes, during the heavy nutting season in September and October.

But, inspite of all this, Hondor and Subu were as different as night and day.

Hondor was the kind of squirrel whose main concern in life was to take care of himself and his family. His motto was "Family Comes First."

Hondor's family had the biggest and the finest nest in town. His wife wore the most expensive clothes and his children had more toys than any of the other squirrel kids around.

When Hondor went to church, which wasn't very often, because he was always busy adding something new onto the house or taking the kids camping, he would put only the small leftover nuts in the offering plate. He always said to himself, "Someday I'll put in bigger nuts, but now I've got to save my nuts so the kids can go to college, and so Hildeen and I can retire on a pecan ranch in California."

(Hildeen was Hondor's wife. Remember, I told you squirrels have strange names.)

Subu, on the other hand, was the kind of squirrel who was concerned as much about others as he was about himself and his family. His motto was, "We are all family." And he lived accordingly.

Subu and his wife Arvella had a small, but comfortable, nest. Their kids didn't have a lot of toys but, they were happy with the ones they had.

They were not an overly religious family but they went to church every Sunday and they always gave generously when the offering plate was passed. Subu thought it was important to give in proportion to what God gave them. If the family collected 500 nuts in a week, they put 50 of the biggest ones in the offering plate. It wasn't that Subu wasn't concerned about the future, like Hondor was, for he also saved nuts for college and retirement. It was just that Subu knew he didn't have to do everything for himself. He had his friends in the church, and he trusted God.

One fall, the weather squirrel predicted a long hard winter. He said it would be the coldest and the snowiest winter in history. That year, all of the squirrels in town worked twice as hard gathering nuts for the long winter. Subu organized a group at church to collect extra nuts for the sick and elderly squirrels who couldn't gather nuts for themselves. They delivered the nuts to the hospitals, the nursing homes, and to all the shut-ins.

All of the squirrels gave generously to the nut fund. That is, all except Hondor. He said, "Check with me next spring. If I have plenty of nuts for my family, then perhaps I'll give some to the nut fund."

Hondor worked around the clock gathering nuts. He filled one store room with nuts and added on another, bigger one which he filled even fuller, just to be safe.

Come February, there was the biggest blizzard the town had ever seen. The snow was so deep, and so heavy, that Hondor's store houses and half his nest came tumbling down out of the tree. Several of the other nests in town were damaged, too, but Hondor's was the worst. His family lost all of their nuts, and they didn't have any place to live.

When Subu found out, he invited Hondor's family to come stay with them until their nest was rebuilt. He also went around to all of the other squirrel families and took up a nut collection. When he was finished, Hondor's family had more nuts than they had had before.

The next Sunday, Hondor, Hildeen and the kids all went to church. When Pastor Squirrely asked for the sharing of joys and prayer concerns, Hondor got up and thanked everyone for everything they had done for them. He said he was thankful for friends like them. And then he said something that surprised everyone, especially Hildeen. He said, "I've got a new motto, we are all family."

When the offering plate was passed that day, Hondor put in more than a tenth of the nuts that had been given to him. And when it came time for prayer, Hondor bowed his head and thanked God for taking care of him and his family.

Home Town Apocalypse

. . . in those days after that tribulation, the sun will be darkened, and the moon will not give its light, and the stars will be falling from the heavens, and the powers in the heavens will be shaken.

But of that day or that hour no one knows, not even the angels in heaven, nor the Son, but only the Father. Take heed, watch, for you do not know when the time will come.

Mark 13:24, 32-33

When I was growing up there was a boy in our church, several years older than I, who was a favorite of all the children and, I think, the adults too. His name was Joe Hanko. Everyone called him Joey. Joey always had a smile for everyone. He was good to us little kids. He loved to give pig-back rides and to play softball with us behind the church. Joey was never mean to us in any way as big boys can sometimes be. If anyone would have asked us, "Which student in your Sunday School best exemplifies the teachings of Jesus?" everyone would have pointed to Joey.

The same attitude prevailed among his classmates and teachers in the high school where he attended. On class night in his senior year Joey received the four year good citizen award for the Weston High School Class of 1963. The teachers said later that when it came time to take the vote, it was unanimous; everyone said it shall be Joe Hanko.

Joe was a good student, excelling in English. His teachers often commented on his stories and poems. But the academic life was not for him. His friends used to say that Joe was a farmer inside and out, and that is what he planned to do after graduation.

Joe was also mechanically inclined and was especially good at making things that were useful on the farm. I remember one occasion when our family visited the Hanko farm for some kind of Sunday afternoon gathering. Joe took us kids out to the machine shed to see the model farm he had designed. It was complete with all of the buildings, a tin roof for the barn, and a round silo made with real cement that Joe had mixed himself. Then he showed us something that I will never forget. It was a farm kid's dream, a toy hay baler he had made with his own hands that actually baled hay like a real baler.

When Joe graduated from high school in late May of the next spring, everyone in our little community rejoiced with his family. We were all proud of Joe. We knew he was a young man who was going to go far.

About three weeks later a neighbor stopped by after morning chores and before he had even gotten out of the car he said, "Did you hear about Joey Hanko? He drowned last night up at Lee Lake." He told us that Joe and some friends had decided to go for a swim after haying all day. Joe developed a cramp and went under before anyone could reach him. They dived and dived but didn't find him until it was too late.

The whole community was in shock. No one could believe it. For his family and all of us who loved him it felt like the end of the world. The story of the drowning was recounted again and again. Everyone wondered how it could have happened to such a strong boy and good swimmer like Joe. Could anything have been done to prevent it? Did they eat before they went in? Who called the sheriff's office? How long did it take for the ambulance to arrive? Every detail was weighed and examined. It was a way of coming to grips with a horrible reality. One of the best and most loved among us was dead.

I remember that one could still see the shock etched on people's faces as they came soberly into the church on the day of the funeral. Joe's family appeared almost numb, their faces drained of all color. They leaned on each other as they made their way up the aisle to the extra row of folding chairs that had been set up in front of the first pew. The church was packed. Every seat was taken and people were standing in the back of the santuary and in the side annex which was opened up for just such occasions. Outside cars were parked tightly in front and behind the church. And across the state highway that runs through the village they were lined up bumper to bumper all the way around the block on both sides of the street.

I don't remember anything about the service except that about half way through a great storm struck. It was one of those fierce summer thunder storms that comes up suddenly without warning. The sky turned black; the wind roared and whistled and very soon after it started, the electricity went off so that the church was almost completely dark. There were several lightning strikes apparently very near the church judging by how quickly they were followed by cracking thunder which shook the building like a sonic boom. This all happened in a matter of minutes and then the rain came in torrents. It was like a dam had burst in the heavens and let a great flood of waters pour down on the roof of our little church.

It stopped as suddenly as it began. A calm followed, a holy stillness, like the peace that comes to one in the midst of grief when there are no more tears to be shed. The storm had vented the outrage that we all felt at this brutal assault on our happy existence.

When we went outside after the service, we were startled to discover that the giant cottonwood tree across the highway from the church had been blown over during the storm and had smashed two of the cars parked beneath it. But that was only a small sample of the storm's devastation. Upon our return to the farm we found acre after acre of corn and oats flattened by the wind. Part of the roof was gone from the barn and in the woods several large trees had been uprooted. The storm had left a mark on our world that would last for a long time to come.

The Hanko family was in church the following Sunday in their usual pew. I don't know how. I don't know if I would have been able to come, but they were there that Sunday and every Sunday after to take their places among the faithful in Christ's church.

The Most Pop In The County

. . . I will gather the remnant of my flock out of all the countries where I have driven them, and I will bring them back to their fold, and they shall be fruitful and multiply. I will set shepherds over them who will care for them, and they shall fear no more, nor be dismayed, neither shall any be missing, says the Lord.

Jeremiah 22:3-4

I grew up on a dairy farm in southwest Wisconsin near the village of Loyd. Nowadays Loyd is not much more than a stop in the road. There are a little over a dozen houses, the township hall, the church, a cemetery up on the hill where my grandparents are buried and little else. But in the days of my youth, there was a one room grade school where I went through all eight grades, a blacksmith shop, a cheese factory, two gas stations and a grocery store.

One of my favorite places in Loyd was Orrin's gas station. Orrin and Clara Fuller lived in a big white house across the highway from the church. At least I remember it as being big. Now that I think about it, it probably wasn't all that big. They used to let us play softball in their yard during Bible School week every summer. I remember because a little stream ran along the edge of the yard and we were continually retrieving the ball from the water. There was a giant cottonwood tree in the corner that we used for a backstop behind home plate. It was blown down one summer day during a fierce thunder storm and smashed a couple of cars that were parked beneath it. It happened while we were all in church at Joey Hanko's funeral, but that's another story.

Clara Fuller was one of the mainstays of our little congregation. She was always there to help whatever the need. She and Orrin were the custodians for a while. The church had a wood furnace and they were the ones who went over very early on winter Sunday mornings to get the fire going. Clara sat in the same spot in the same pew every Sunday — on the left side, in the back of the sanctuary, on the end of the pew near the aisle. She was usually the first one in her place on Sunday morning at eleven o'clock.

I remember Clara best with her arms full of pies on her way across the street to help get ready for a church supper — dark blue print dress, black square-heeled shoes, hair in a bun, a big smile and a snappy hello — that was Clara, one of the saints of the church. It was because of Clara, and a lot of folks like her, that I came to love the church.

Orrin never went to church much, at least I don't remember ever seeing him there except maybe at a supper or a funeral. He ran the filling station on the north edge of town. He took over the station right after Orrie Frye died.

I'll never forget Orrie. He had braces on his legs, the result of a bout with polio when he was still a young man. He moved around the station on crutches. It always amazed me that he could get around so well and do as much as he did, handicapped as he was.

Everybody was afraid that the station would be closed after Orrie died and it was closed for a while. Then Orrin and Clara bought it from the Frye family and the whole community breathed a sigh of relief. The station was open again and it wasn't too difficult to get used to saying Orrin's instead of Orrie's.

Unlike Orrie, Orrin was able to do a little mechanical work. He opened up the garage part of the station where he sharpened sickles and tinkered with lawn mowers and chainsaws. He did some welding, a little forge work, as well as changing oil and other light service work on cars and tractors. He had a pretty good bicycle business, too.

My brothers and my sister and I used to take our bicycle tires in regularly for repairs. If it was a big job, Orrin would say, "Leave it here and pick it up in a couple of days." If it was just a patch or a leaky valve stem, he would stop what he was doing and fix it on the spot. When he was finished, he would roll it out and we would say, "How much do we owe you?" Orrin would look at us like he hadn't noticed who we were before and he'd say, "Oh, about a quarter," or if it had been a big job, he would say, "Oh, about a dollar." There was never any fixed price. The charge was always, "Oh about," which amounted to whatever Orrin thought we kids could afford.

As well as being a filling station and a fix-it shop, Orrin's was a kind of gathering place, mostly for the men of the community. A woman might stop in to get some gas (those were the days when you still heard people say, "Give me a dollar's worth," and you could go a long way on a dollar's worth), but you hardly ever saw a woman sit down and drink a bottle of pop. That may have been because there were no chairs at Orrin's except the one that Orrin sat on over by the cash register. There were tires and pop crates — and that's where the men would sit and visit when they came in to have a pop. Boys stood up. That was the difference between men and boys.

In the winter time the circle would be around the potbellied stove which sat to the side near the center of the room. In warm weather you would find the men over by the pop and ice cream cooler. It was one of the old chest types. If you sat near enough, you could feel a blast of cold air when someone reached in to get a Popsicle. There were sometimes as many as ten or twelve men sitting around in the late afternoon or early evening, having a pop and shooting the breeze. The milk haulers, Junior Ripley and Bill Brown, big strapping guys who could lift a ten-gallon milkcan over their heads in each hand, would be there on their way home from work. Larry Fuller would stop on the way down from the ridge with a load of hay. Frank Brown, our cattle trucker, on his way back from the stock yards, Art Travis, the town fix-it man and fence builder, Johnny Ironmonger, the township grader man, old Mr. French, the retired blacksmith, Buford Frye, Ed Swenick, Fred Soul, Albert Crary, Donny Moore, Alphie Hanold, Archie Sumwalt, young men and old; they would all be there in their usual places. They would talk about the price of feeder-pigs or who had gotten caught watering down their milk that year. Sometimes old Mr. French would tell about the time the gypsies passed through town and lifted his gold watch.

They used to say that Orrin sold more pop than anybody else in the county and I guess maybe it was true. It wasn't until years later that I realized that they didn't really come there for the pop. They could have drunk pop anywhere. There were other places in town where you could buy pop. They could have drunk pop at home. They came to Orrin's because he made them welcome. It was a place to lay their burdens down.

Orrin was a quiet fellow, not outgoing or affable in any remarkable way. I don't remember him ever telling a funny story or a joke. On occasion he could be a bit of a grouch. But he was in his own unassuming way one of God's own faithful shepherds. He provided a place where we could get what we needed. They, (and I should say we, because I include myself in that number even though I was just a kid), found something there which all of us long for in the depths of our hearts, a community where we belonged, a resting place in the warm company of friends.

Notes

[1] Frederick Buechner, *Telling the Truth, The Gospel As Tragedy, Comedy and Fairy Tale*, (San Francisco, Harper & Row, 1977), pp. 16 & 17.

[2] *Ibid.*

[3] Fred B. Craddock, *Overhearing the Gospel*, (Nashville, Abingdon Press, 1978), p. 140.

[4] Michael Goldberg, *Theology & Narrative: A Critical Introduction*, (Nashville, Abingdon Press, 1981), p. 39.

[5] Michael Williams, *Friends for Life*, (Nashville, Abingdon Press, 1989), p. 10.

[6] Thomas E. Boomershine, *Story Journey*, (Nashville, Abingdon Press, 1988), p. 17.

[7] William J. Bausch, *Storytelling: Imagination and Faith*, (Mystic, Twenty-third Publications, 1984), p. 17.

[8] *Chicago Tribune*, August 13, 1988.

[9] Phillips Brooks, et.al., "O Little Town of Bethlehem," *The United Methodist Hymnal*, (Nashville, The United Methodist Publishing House, 1989), p. 230.

[10] Christina G. Rossetti, "In the Bleak Midwinter," *The United Methodist Hymnal*, (Nashville, The United Methodist Publishing House, 1989), p. 221.

[11] *The United Methodist Hymnal*, (Nashville, The United Methodist Publishing House, 1989), pp. 41 & 42.

[12] *The United Methodist Hymnal*, (Nashville, The United Methodist Publishing House, 1989), p. 711.

REPRINTS

The following stories appeared, or are scheduled to appear in "Seasons: The Inter-Faith Family Journal," Inter-Faith Committee on the Family, Box 2018, Milwaukee, Wis. 53201, and are reprinted here with permission.

(1) "Help Me Get Home," *Seasons 8:1* (Spring 1989), p. 17.

(2) "A Distant Triumph Song," *Seasons 8:3* (Fall 1989), pp. 17f.

(3) "The Church in Need of Aid," *Seasons 8:4* (Winter 1989), pp. 16f.

(4) "Old Farmer," *Seasons 9:1* (Spring 1990), pp. 17f.

(5) "In the Bleak Midwinter: An R-Rated Christmas Story," forthcoming in *Seasons 9:2* (Summer 1990).

(6) "Where the Story Never Ends," forthcoming in *Seasons 9:4* (Winter 1990).